> *The only way to improve your business is to know your numbers.*
>
> — Marcus Lemonis

Table Of Contents

Copyright @2024 and Disclaimer

Forward

Magic of Accounting, By Rennie Thangiah

In preparing this publication, Rennie Thangiah has provided a real service to those who find themselves between having a rudimentary knowledge of accounting and those possessing the skills to effortlessly produce a full set of detailed and complex accounts.

Rennie has covered the entire spectrum in a practical and concise manner, offering multiple detailed examples that guide the reader through financial transactions step-by-step, leading to their ultimate conclusion in a final set of accounts.

The method of presenting various subjects is particularly helpful, with explanations followed by worked examples. These are further supported by test questions, providing the reader with the opportunity to practice their recent learnings and observe their outcomes. Additionally, there are various cross-references to websites that further assist the reader.

With the proliferation of "automated" accounting software (e.g., Xero and MYOB), there is a potential for users of these systems to grasp the necessary processes without appreciating the detailed impact on either the accounts or the business in which they are engaged. Once again, this is where "Magic of Accounting" assists users in understanding the full impacts of their entries and the use of automated accounting systems on business outcomes.

In conclusion, this one inexpensive publication has covered all matters accounting, offering invaluable assistance to a range of potential users, from business proprietors to clerical assistants to those just starting an accounting career.

I highly recommend this publication.

Arthur Huxtable, CPA SIA ACIS

Acknowledgements

This book would not have been possible without the support and inspiration of many individuals. First and foremost, I want to acknowledge Arthur Huxtable FCPA SIA ACIS, whose dedication to educating managers at Stellar Call Centres ignited a passion in me to make accounting accessible and engaging for everyone. Arthur, your footsteps have guided me, and your encouragement has fueled my commitment to this lifelong mission of educating non-accountants.

Arthur's extensive experience in senior finance positions and his transition to founding his own practice, Huxtable & Co, has been a beacon of inspiration. His role as a Certified Practicing Accountant (CPA) and various esteemed positions within the financial community have not only enriched my understanding but also demonstrated the profound impact one can have in this field.

Thank you, Arthur, for planting the seed of passion within me. Your mentorship and unwavering support have been instrumental in my journey, and I am deeply grateful for your influence in making this book a reality.

Thank you, Alex Tian, CPA for your comprehensive review of this book, despite your incredibly busy schedules, your expertise and insights have been instrumental in enhancing the quality and clarity of this work. Your dedication and support are deeply appreciated.

To all my readers, I hope this book serves as a valuable resource in your quest to understand and navigate the world of accounting with confidence and clarity.

With heartfelt gratitude,
Rennie Thangiah

Arthur has held a variety of senior finance positions with large organisations in the communications, manufacturing and service industries leaving the Stellar Group as Chief Financial Officer to commence his own accounting and tax practice as Huxtable & Co in 2012 while retaining various Board positions both with Stellar and other entities. Arthur is a Certified Practicing Accountant (CPA), a member of the Chartered Governance Institute of Australia, a, member of the Financial Services Institute of Australasia, a registered Tax Agent and holds a CPA Practicing Certificate.

About the Author

Rennie Thangiah is an accomplished finance professional with over 15 years of experience across a diverse range of industries. His career spans senior roles in sectors including travel, pharmaceuticals, services, FMCG, SaaS, telecommunications, and media. Rennie has a proven track record of driving financial strategy, leveraging data-driven insights, and fostering collaborative leadership.

Rennie has held pivotal positions such as Chief Financial Officer at Cruiseco Ltd in the travel industry, and Pharmacy Phusion in the pharmaceutical sector. His expertise extends to serving as Financial Controller at Rentokil Initial, a services company, and Group Reporting Manager at Coca-Cola Amatil in the FMCG industry. Rennie also brought his financial acumen to the SaaS industry, with roles at Integrated Research and Information Resources.

In addition to his extensive professional experience, Rennie has contributed to major projects as a consultant for prominent organizations including Obela Fresh Dips & Spreads, Telstra Corporation, and Channel Nine. His ability to streamline financial processes, implement new systems, and lead high-performing teams has been a hallmark of his career. Rennie is a Certified Practicing Accountant (CPA) and holds an MBA from the University of Hull, UK. He is also a member of the Chartered Institute of Management Accountants (CIMA), demonstrating his commitment to professional excellence and continuous learning. With a passion for making complex financial concepts accessible, Rennie has dedicated himself to educating and empowering non-accountants through his work, including the creation of engaging and informative resources such as this book. His dedication to the field of accounting and finance is matched only by his enthusiasm for helping others understand and succeed in this critical domain.

Stay Connected and Let's Grow Together:

I would love to stay connected with you beyond this book. I invite you to connect with me on LinkedIn at **https://www.linkedin.com/in/renniethangiah/**. Through LinkedIn, we can continue to exchange ideas, insights, and grow our professional networks together. When connecting, please mention that you have purchased my book.

Additionally, if you are looking to enhance your team's understanding of accounting in a way that's directly relevant to your business, I am available to provide tailored training sessions. Whether it's demystifying complex accounting concepts or offering practical applications based on your organisation's needs, I'm here to help. Please feel free to message me on LinkedIn to discuss how we can collaborate.

Looking forward to connecting and working together to elevate your team's financial acumen.

Part 1 - Introduction to Accounting

Welcome to the world of accounting! In this part, you'll embark on a journey to uncover why accounting is the backbone of every successful business. We start with simple, relatable examples like deciding between depositing money in a bank or launching your own T-shirt business. Through these scenarios, you'll discover the essential role that accounting plays in tracking business transactions and producing crucial financial reports. It's not just about numbers; it's about telling the story of your business, and this part lays the foundation for understanding that narrative.

Chapter 01: Need for Accounting

Chapter 01 Objective: Understand why accounting is essential for businesses by exploring scenarios of depositing money in a bank vs starting a business, highlighting the importance of tracking business transactions and maintaining proper financial records.

Consider the following scenario: Meet Jim. He has saved up some money and wants to use it to make more money. He has two choices:

1. Deposit the money in a bank and earn interest.
2. Start his own business.

Deposit money in the bank, which is much easier to track.

Let's first examine the bank option. If Jim deposits his money in a bank, he will earn extra money, which is called interest. It's easy for him to see how much he's made just by looking at his bank statement. A bank statement is an official summary of financial transactions occurring within a given period for each bank account held by a person or business with a financial institution. This is also the least risky option; therefore, it returns much less.

MAGIC BANK

675 Tricks Street, PO BOX 4000
VictoriaBC V8Y 34W 1-800 555 7777

INVESTMENT ACCOUNT STATEMENT
Page: 1 of 1

JIM INVESTOR
123 Maple Street, Sunnyville, NSW 888, Australia

Statement period	Account No.
1/01/2027 to 31/01/2027	0005-123-781

Date	Description	Ref.	Withdrawals	Deposits	Balance
2/01/2027	Depost			10,000.00	10,000.00
2/02/2027	Bank Charges	1002	5.00		9,995.00
2/02/2027	Interest Income	1025		41.67	10,036.67
2/02/2027	Interest	2522			
	Totals		5.00	10,041.67	

The interest rate used in the example is 5% per annum. In the example, Jim deposits $10,000, the bank charges $5 per month as fees using the bank account. Interest received for the month of January 2027 is $41.67. The profit on the deposit for January 2027 is $41.67 less $5.00 = $36.67. Profit Margin is 0.37% ($36.67/$10,000).

Investment	$	10,000.00		Interest Rate	5%
Interest Income	$	41.67			
Less Bank Charges	-$	5.00			
Profit	$	36.67			
Profit Margin		0.37%	<--- $37/ $10,000		

The Challenge of Tracking Business Transactions.

Now, let's think about if Jim decides to start a business because he is passionate about selling T-shirts and he believes he can generate better returns although it is riskier than investing with a Bank. Jim believes he can make at least a 10% Return.

Business transactions are not easy to keep track of, that is why accounting is required. Furthermore, businesses need to maintain proper financial records and produce reports for use by regulators, customers, suppliers, financial institutions, and the business itself.

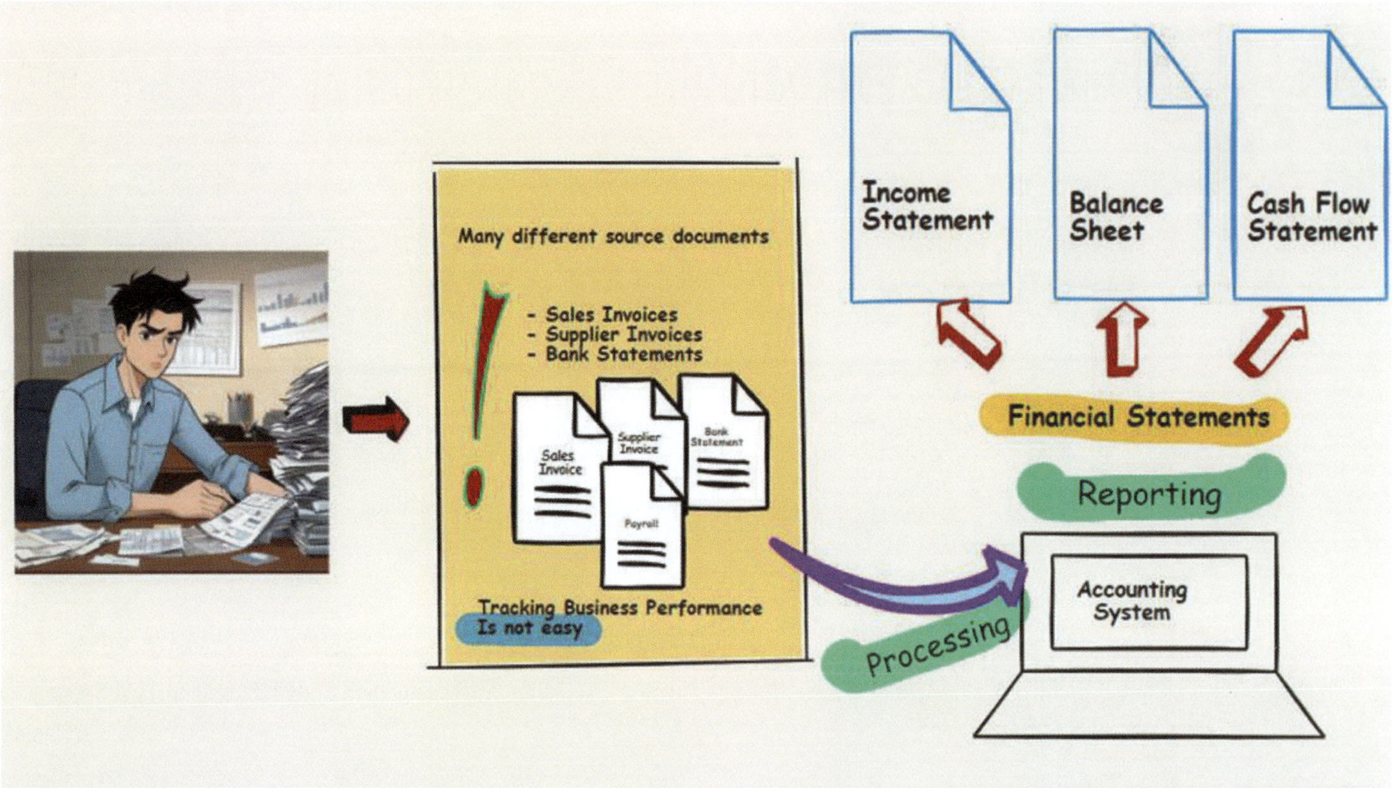

Running a business means Jim will have many different transactions, like buying stuff he needs, paying for advertising, and maybe buying materials if he's making something to sell. Knowing how well his business is doing can be hard without a systematic process to document business transactions. The process of documenting and reporting on financial transactions is called accounting. Knowing how to read and understand financial reports makes it possible to ascertain whether a business is achieving its target returns, is in trouble, is growing or shrinking.

Chapter 01: Skill-Building Exercises and Questions

It is useful to understand the purpose of your business to understand how accounting reports on it. Please answer the following questions. If you are not employed or don't own a business, pick a company of your choice.

Question 1: What services or products does your business/the business you work for provide?

Question 2: Where did the passion and vision come from to start the business?

Question 3 (Select the correct Answer)
(explanation to correct answer in Appendix 4).

What is the primary reason Jim needs accounting for his T-shirt business?

A. To track the bank interest on his savings

B. To easily determine the number of T-shirts he sold

C. To maintain proper financial records and produce reports for stakeholders

D. To avoid paying taxes

Well done! You have learned about the necessity of accounting in tracking business transactions, maintaining financial records, and producing reports essential for various stakeholders.

Chapter 02: What is Accounting?

Chapter 02 Objective: Gain a foundational understanding of accounting, including its purpose, key financial statements, and the role of financial statements for various stakeholders.

Accounting is often considered the language of business.

It is beneficial to grasp basic accounting, as it is the universally accepted language for reporting on business performance.

Identify financial business events.

Financial business events are occurrences that affect the financial position or performance of a business. These events are the raw data that are process and sometimes adjusted to provide business insights. Identifying these events accurately is the first step in the accounting process. Examples of financial business events include:

Sales Transactions: Selling goods or services to customers.

Purchase Transactions: Buying supplies, inventory, or services.

Financing Transactions: Borrowing or repaying loans, issuing shares, etc.

Each of these events needs to be identified and recorded to reflect the true financial health of the business.

Process and Summarise Financial Transactions

Once financial events are identified, they need to be recorded systematically. This involves:

Recording: Each event is recorded as a transaction in the accounting system. This step involves a combination of bank transactions and journal entries, where each transaction is noted with its corresponding debit and credit.

Debits and credits are basic accounting principles.
Debits: Money going into an account (like adding money).
Credits: Money going out of an account (like spending money).
Example:
Buying supplies: Debit (increases) supplies account, Credit (decreases) cash account.
Each transaction affects two accounts, keeping the books balanced.

Classifying: Transactions are classified into categories such as assets, liabilities, equity, revenues, and expenses, based on the chart of accounts.

Transactions: Any business activities that involve money being exchanged, such as buying, selling, or paying bills.
Categories:
Assets: Things the business owns that have value, like cash, equipment, or buildings.
Liabilities: Debts or obligations the business owes to others, like loans or accounts payable.
Equity: The owner's share of the business after all liabilities are subtracted from assets. It represents the owner's stake in the company.
Revenues: Money the business earns from its normal operations, like sales or service fees.
Expenses: Costs incurred by the business in the process of earning revenue, like rent, salaries, and utilities.
Chart of Accounts: A list of all the accounts a company uses to keep track of its financial transactions, organized by categories.

Summarising: Classified transactions are summarised into accounts, showing their cumulative effect of the transactions over a period.

These steps transform raw financial data into structured information, making it easier to analyse and report on businesses.

Produce Financial Statements

Financial statements refer to 3 main reports that are produced to assess various aspects of financial performance of a business. The three main reports are:

Balance Sheet: This report provides a snapshot of the business's financial position at a specific point in time. It shows what the business owns (assets), what it owes (liabilities), and the owners' equity.

Income Statement: Also known as the profit and loss statement, this report shows the business's performance over a specific period. It details revenues, expenses, and the resulting profit or loss.

Profit or Loss: Profit: The amount of money a business has left after subtracting all its expenses from its total revenues. It indicates financial gain. Loss: When a business's expenses exceed its revenues, resulting in a negative financial outcome.

Cash Flow Statement: This report tracks the flow of cash in and out of the business over a period. It highlights the business's operating, investing, and financing activities, showing how cash is generated and used.

Users of Financial Statements.

Financial statements are essential information about a company's financial health.

Various users rely on these statements to make informed decisions:

Investors: Use financial statements to evaluate profitability and growth potential to make investment decisions.

Creditors and Lenders: Assess a company's creditworthiness and ability to repay loans.

Management: Monitor performance, plan strategies, and make operational decisions.

Employees and Labour Unions: Gauge company stability and profitability for wage negotiations and job security.

Regulatory Agencies: Ensure compliance with regulations and standards.

Suppliers and Trade Creditors: Evaluate the creditworthiness of customers.

Customers: Ensure the company's stability for long-term contracts.

Government and Tax Authorities: Calculate taxes and monitor compliance with tax laws.

Public and Community: Assess the company's economic contributions and ethical practices.

By understanding these users, companies can ensure that their financial reporting meets the needs of all stakeholders, promoting transparency and informed decision-making.

Chapter 02: Skill-Building Exercises and Questions

Exercise : Identifying Financial Business Events in your business or the business you work for.

Sales business events. What does the business sell? Who are the customers?

Products and / or Services?

Who are the Customers?

Who uses the business's financial information:?

Well done! You have gained a foundational understanding of accounting, its purpose, and the key financial statements used to assess a business's financial health.

Chapter 03: Financial Statements, The Three Primary Reports

Chapter 03 Objective: Learn about the three primary financial reports—Income Statement, Balance Sheet, and Cash Flow Statement—and their importance in assessing a business's financial health.

The term "Financial Statements" collectively refers to the three main financial reports. Each of these reports is related and provides insights into various aspects of the financial health of a business.

Income Statement: shows how much profit a business made and spent over a specific period of time.

Balance Sheet: Provides a snapshot of what the business owns and owes at a specific point in time.

Cash Flow Statement: Tracks the cash movement in and out of the business.

These reports together give a comprehensive view of the business's financial health. Let's discuss these reports in more detail.

Income Statement

Tees and Giggles Ltd

Income Statement

	Period 1
Date From	01-Jan-27
Date To	31-Jan-27
Sales Revenue	5,400
Cost of Sales	(4,500)
Gross Profit	**900**
Gross Profit Margin %	**17%**
Expenses	
Wages Expense	0
Wages Oncosts Expense	0
Electricity Expense	0
Rent Expense	(200)
Advertising Expense	0
Subscription Expense	0
Depreciation Expense	0
Total Expenses	**(200)**
Earning Before Interest and Taxation (EBIT)	**700**
EBIT Margin	**13%**
Interest Expense	0
Profit Before Tax (PBT)	**700**
Profit Before Tax Margin	**13%**
Income Tax Expense	**(210)**
Profit (-Loss) After Tax (PAT)	**490**
Profit (-Loss) After Tax %	**9%**

What Information Can you Get:

The Income Statement, also known as the Profit and Loss Statement, tells you whether your business made a profit or a loss during a specific period. It lists all the revenues (money earned) and expenses (money spent). The difference between the total revenue and total expenses is your net profit or loss.

Key Components:

•Revenues: Money earned from sales of goods or services.
•Expenses: Costs incurred to run the business, such as rent, utilities, and salaries.
•Profit or Loss: Revenues minus expenses.

Why it Matters:

• Helps you see if your business is profitable.
• Revenue details and expense breakdowns.
• Provides insight into cost management and pricing strategies.

Balance Sheet

Tees and Giggles Ltd	
Balance Sheet	**Period 1**
As At	**31-Jan-27**
Assets	
Current Assets	
Cash	11,200
Inventory/Stock	500
Accounts Receivable	0
Prepaid Expenses	0
Total Current Assets	**11,700**
Fixed Assets	
Fixed Assets	0
Accumulated Depreciation	0
Total Fixed Assets	**0**
Total Assets	**11,700**
Current Liabilities	
Accounts Payable	0
Deferred Revenue	0
Accrued Employee Costs	0
Provision for Income Tax	(210)
Total Current Liabilities	**(210)**
Long Term Liabilities	
Bank Loans	(1,000)
Total Liabilities	**(1,210)**
Net Assets	**10,490**
Equity	
Share Capital	10,000
Retained Earnings b/f	0
Retained Earnings	490
Total Equity	**10,490**

What Information Can you Get:

The Balance Sheet gives a snapshot of your business's financial position at a specific point in time. It lists all your assets (what you own), liabilities (what you owe), and equity (owner's interest in the business).

Key Components:

- Assets: Everything the business owns, such as cash, inventory, and equipment.
- Liabilities: Everything the business owes, like loans and accounts payable.
- Equity: The owner's interest in the business, which is the assets minus liabilities.

Why it Matters:

- Shows the financial stability of your business.
- Helps you understand the value of what you own versus what you owe.
- Useful for securing loans or attracting investors.

Cash Flow Statement

Tees and Giggles Ltd	
Statement of Cash Flows	Period 1
Date From	01-Jan-27
Date To	31-Jan-27
Operating Cash	
Receipts from Customers	5,400
Payments to Staff	0
Payments to Suppliers	(5,200)
Loan Interest Payment	0
Income Taxes Paid	0
Net Operating Cash	**200**
Investing	
Payments for Fixed Assets	0
Financing	
Cash from Shareholders	10,000
Dividend Paid	0
Bank Loans Received	1,000
Loan Principle Repayments	0
Net Cash for The Period	**11,200**
Opening Cash	**0**
Closing Cash	**11,200**

What Information Can you Get:

The Cash Flow Statement tracks the flow of cash in and out of your business over a period, i.e., it explains how the cash balance in the Balance Sheet was arrived at. It shows how well your business generates cash to pay its debts, fund its operating expenses, and invest in growth.

Key Components:

- Operating Activities: Cash generated from day-to-day business operations.
- Investing Activities: Cash used for buying or selling assets like equipment or investments.
- Financing Activities: Cash received from or paid to financiers, such as loans and equity contributions.

Why it Matters:

- Helps you understand how well your business manages its cash.
- Shows details about how cash is being received and being spent.
- Crucial for planning and ensuring liquidity.

Chapter 03: Skill-Building Exercises and Questions

Exercise 1: Please get a copy of your business's most up-to-date financial statements. Your accountant or CFO will be able to help you with this. If the financial statements are not available, please obtain a copy of your favourite publicly listed business. You can search Google for websites where you can obtain publicly listed financial statements. Update the following table.

Total Revenue

Net Profit After Tax

Total Assets

Total Liabilities

Net Assets

Closing Cash Balance

Exercise 2 : Multiple Choice Questions (Select the correct Answer) (explanation to correct answer in Appendix 4).

Q1 - Which financial statement provides a snapshot of a business's financial position at a specific point in time?

A. Income Statement

B. Balance Sheet

C. Cash Flow Statement

D. Statement of Retained Earnings

Q2 - What does the Income Statement show?

A. The financial position of the business

B. The cash inflows and outflows over a period

C. The revenues, expenses, and profit or loss over a period

D. The changes in equity over time

Q3 - Which statement tracks the flow of cash in and out of a business?

A. Income Statement

B. Balance Sheet

C. Cash Flow Statement

D. Statement of Retained Earnings

Q4 - Why are financial statements important for investors?

A. To ensure compliance with tax laws

B. To evaluate profitability and growth potential

C. To track day-to-day operational activities

D. To determine employee salaries

Q5 - What does the Balance Sheet typically include?

A. Revenues and expenses

B. Cash inflows and outflows

C. Assets, liabilities, and equity

D. Sales and purchases

Well done! You explored the three main financial statements—Income Statement, Balance Sheet, and Cash Flow Statement—and their roles in providing a comprehensive view of a business's financial status.

Chapter 04: Producing and Interpreting Financial Statements

Chapter 04 Objective: Understand how financial statements are produced through the accounting process, including recording, classifying, and summarising financial transactions and interpreting each report. Knowing how financial statements are produced helps you work better with your accounting team or accountant.

Now that you are familiar with the report layout, let's examine how the reports are generated using five business events in a fictitious company called Tees and Giggles Ltd. Tees and Giggles Ltd is in the business of selling T-shirts with funny prints.

Five Business Events.

Five Business Events

Tees and Giggles Ltd

Event No.	Date	Description	Amount
1	1/01/2027	Transfer cash from personal account to the business account.	$10,000
		The business issues share cetficate as evidence of ownership	
2	1/01/2027	Borrow money from the bank.	$ 1,000
		Bank issues Loan Agreement	
3	1/01/2027	Purchase T-shirts	
		Supplier issues payables invoice	
		Number of units	1,000
		Cost per unit ($ Each)	$ 5
		Credit Terms Days	10
		Total Cost	$ 5,000
4	1/01/2027	Sell T-Shirts	
		Business issues sales invoice to purchaser.	
		Number of T-shirts	900
		Markup on Cost	20%
		Sales price per Unit ($ Each)	$ 6
		Credit Terms Days	10
		Total Sales Value	$ 5,400
5	1/01/2027	Pay rent for the month	
		Land Lord issues lease agreement and Invoice	
		Rent amount ($)	$ 200
		Credit Terms Days	10
		Income Tax Rate	0%

The Accounting Equation.

The principles of the Accounting Equation is used when processing financial transactions.

The accounting equation is also fundamental to understanding financial accounting and financial reporting.

The equation's history dates back to the 15th century when Italian mathematician and Franciscan friar Luca Pacioli introduced the concept in his seminal work "Summa de Arithmetica, Geometria, Proportioni et Proportionalità," published in 1494. Pacioli's book laid the foundation for double-entry bookkeeping, revolutionising the way businesses recorded and reported their financial transactions. His work highlighted the importance of balancing assets and liabilities to determine a company's equity, ensuring accuracy and transparency in financial reporting.

The accounting equations states that:

Assets - Liabilities = Equity (or Assets = Equity + Liabilities)

This equation ensures that a company's financial statements are balanced and accurately and completely reflect its financial position.

Equity, from a business owner's perspective, represents the portion of the business that the owner possesses. It is the residual value of the business once all debts and liabilities have been deducted from the business's assets.

Think of it this way:

Assets: Everything your business owns (cash, equipment, property).

Liabilities: Everything your business owes (loans, bills, salaries).

Equity: The residual interest of owners. i.e. What's left over when you subtract liabilities from assets, this is represented by Initial Capital Contribution + Profit Generated by the Business.

Equity increase as the business becomes more profitable. Thus, equity serves as a key measure of the business's financial health.

Transaction Number	2
Description	Borrow from bank

Explanation

The business takes a loan of $1,000 from the bank. This transaction increases the business's cash assets (as the money is received from the bank) and also increases its liabilities (as the business now owes $1,000 to the bank).

Accounting Equation

Assets	+	Liabilities	=	Equity
$1,000		**$1,000**		**$0**

- **Assets** increase by $10,000 (the cash received).
- **Liabilities** remain $0 (no debt or obligations are created).
- **Equity** increases by $10,000 (reflecting the owner's investment in the business).

Transaction Number	3
Description	Purchase of Stock/Inventory

Explanation

The business spends $5,000 from its cash reserves to purchase T-shirts, which are added to its inventory. This transaction exchanges one type of asset (cash) for another type of asset (inventory). Therefore, while the total amount of assets remains the same, the composition of the assets changes.

Accounting Equation

Assets	+	Liabilities	=	Equity
-$5,000 (Cash) **+$5,000 (Inventory)**		**$0**		**$0**

- **Assets** decrease by $5,000 in cash (as the money is spent).
- **Assets** increase by $5,000 in inventory (as the T-shirts are added to stock).
- **Liabilities** remain unchanged at $0.
- **Equity** remains unchanged at $0.

Explanation of the five transactions using the Accounting Equation.

Remember, accounting will treat the business as a separate person/entity.

Before transferring the cash to the business account, the business had no assets or liabilities and, therefore, 0 (zero) equity.

Transaction Number	1
Description	Capital Investment

Explanation

The owner invests $10,000 their personal money into the business. This investment increases the business's cash assets (as the money is deposited into the business's bank account). Since this is an owner's equity investment, no liabilities are created. Instead, the business's equity increases by the same amount.

Accounting Equation

Assets	+	Liabilities	=	Equity
$10,000		**$0**		**$10,000**

Explanation

- **Assets** increase (the cash received).
- **Liabilities** remain $0 (no debt or obligations are created).
- **Equity** increases by $10,000 (reflecting the owner's investment in the business).

Transaction Number	4
Description	Sell T-shirts

Explanation

The business sells T-shirts for a total of $6,000. This transaction increases the business's cash holdings by $6,000 while reducing its inventory. The difference between the sale price and the inventory cost generates a profit, which increases the equity of the business.

Accounting Equation

Assets	+	Liabilities	=	Equity
$6,000		$0		$6,000

- **Assets** increase by $6,000 in cash (from the sales).
- **Liabilities** remain unchanged at $0.
- **Equity** increases by $6,000 (reflecting the profit generated from the sales).

Transaction Number	5
Description	Pay rent for the month

Explanation

The business pays $200 for monthly rent. This transaction decreases the business's cash assets by $200. The rent expense also reduces the business's equity by the same amount, as it is considered an operating expense.

Accounting Equation

Assets	+	**Liabilities**	=	**Equity**
($200)		$0		($200)

- **Assets** decrease by $200 in cash (due to the rent payment).
- **Liabilities** remain unchanged at $0.
- **Equity** decreases by $200 (reflecting the expense incurred).

Although each of the transactions makes sense individually, it is difficult to assess the financial status of the business just by looking at these transactions.

The principles of double-entry are developed into a ledger system to further categorise financial transactions. This enables the production of financial statements that provide better insights into business performance.

The system includes:

1. A classification map called a chart of accounts.

2. And ledgers for Sales, purchases and general ledger

3. And subsidiary registers such as stock/inventory.

Let's look at how we can use a simple chart of accounts to produce financial statements.

As previously discussed, three primary financial statements are used to assess various aspects of business performance.

The Chart of Accounts and Cash Classification.

This is the Chart of Accounts for Tees and Giggles Ltd. We will be coding the transactions arising from the business events using this.

Account codes are used so that they are easier to refer to and categorise in ranges. E.g.

1 = Assets, 2 = Liabilities, 3 = Equity, 4 = Income Statement.

Chart of Accounts, The Classification System

Balance Sheet and Income Statement

Account	Account Description	Category	Report
1000	Cash	Asset	Balance Sheet
1200	T-Shirts	Asset	Balance Sheet
1210	Accounts Receivable	Asset	Balance Sheet
2100	Accounts Payable	Liability	Balance Sheet
2500	Bank Loans	Liability	Balance Sheet
3000	Share Capital	Equity	Balance Sheet
3100	Retained Earnings	Equity	Balance Sheet
4000	Sales Revenue	Income	Income Statement
4100	Cost of Sales	Expense	Income Statement
4200	Rent Expense	Expense	Income Statement

Cash Flow Statement

Cash Analysis	Cash Flow Category
Cash from Owner	Financing Activities
Cash from Loans	Financing Activities
Cash Spent on Stock	Operating Activities
Cash Received from Sales	Operating Activities
Cash Spent on Rent	Operating Activities

How the Chart of Accounts is used for reporting.

Using the above Chart of Accounts, each business transaction is coded as follows and posted in a ledger. Notice that each transaction has a "+" (Debit) and "-" (Credit) number, complying with the Accounting Equation/Double Entry System discussed earlier.

Computerised ledger systems are sophisticated and summarise these transactions under the watchful eyes of your Accountant or accounting team.

Transaction No.		1		
Date		1/01/2027		
Transfer cash from personal account to the business account.				
Account & Description		**Amount**	**Report**	**Cash Analysis**
1000-Cash	$	10,000	Balance Sheet	Cash from Owner
3000-Share Capital	-$	10,000	Balance Sheet	

Transaction No.		2		
Date		1/01/2027		
Borrow money from the bank.				
Account		**Amount**	**Report Row Description**	**Cash Analysis**
1000-Cash	$	1,000	Balance Sheet	Cash from Loans
2500-Bank Loans	-$	1,000	Balance Sheet	

Transaction No.		3		
Date		1/01/2027		
Purchase T-shirts				
Account		**Amount**	**Report Row Description**	**Cash Analysis**
1200-T-Shirts	$	5,000	Balance Sheet	
2100-Accounts Payable	-$	5,000	Balance Sheet	
2100-Accounts Payable	$	5,000	Balance Sheet	
1000-Cash	-$	5,000	Balance Sheet	Cash Spent on Stock

Transaction No.	4		
Date	1/01/2027		
Sell T-shirts			
Account	**Amount**	**Report Row Description**	**Cash Analysis**
1210-Accounts Receivable	$ 5,400	Balance Sheet	
4000-Sales Revenue	-$ 5,400	Income Statement	
1000-Cash	$ 5,400	Balance Sheet	Cash Received from Sales
1210-Accounts Receivable	-$ 5,400	Balance Sheet	
4100-Cost of Sales	$ 4,500	Income Statement	
1200-T-Shirts	-$ 4,500	Balance Sheet	

Transaction No.	5		
Date	1/01/2027		
Pay rent for the month			
Account	**Amount**	**Report Row Description**	**Cash Analysis**
4200-Rent Expense	$ 200	Income Statement	
2100-Accounts Payable	-$ 200	Balance Sheet	
2100-Accounts Payable	$ 200	Balance Sheet	
1000-Cash	-$ 200	Balance Sheet	Cash Spent on Rent

Trial Balance.

A trial balance is a bookkeeping report that lists the balances of all ledger accounts of a business at a specific point in time. It serves as a tool to check the accuracy of the bookkeeping entries and ensure that the total debits equal the total credits, indicating that the accounts are balanced.

Key Points About a Trial Balance

List of Account Balances:

The trial balance includes all the accounts used in the general ledger, which are categorized into assets, liabilities, equity, revenues, and expenses.

Each account is listed with its ending balance, either as a debit or a credit.

Debits and Credits:

In accounting, every transaction affects at least two accounts, maintaining the balance through debits and credits.

Debits and credits must always equal each other for the books to be balanced.

Purpose of a Trial Balance:

Check Accuracy: It helps to verify that all entries in the ledger are correct and that the accounting equation (Assets = Liabilities + Equity) holds true.

Identify Errors: If the total debits do not equal the total credits, it indicates that there might be errors in the bookkeeping entries.

Preparation for Financial Statements: It serves as a preliminary step before preparing formal financial statements like the income statement and balance sheet.

This is the trial balance for Jim's T-shirt business based on the transactions above.

Trial Balance

Trial Balance

Combined	**Report Row**	**Report**	**Debits**	**Credits**	**Balance**
1000-Cash	Cash	Balance Sheet	$ 11,200	$ -	$ 11,200
1200-T-Shirts	T-Shirts	Balance Sheet	$ 500	$ -	$ 500
1210-Accounts Receivable	Accounts Receivable	Balance Sheet	$ -	$ -	$ -
2100-Accounts Payable	Accounts Payable	Balance Sheet	$ -	$ -	$ -
2500-Bank Loans	Bank Loans	Balance Sheet	$ -	$ 1,000	-$ 1,000
3000-Share Capital	Share Capital	Balance Sheet	$ -	$ 10,000	-$ 10,000
3100-Retained Earnings	Retained Earnings	Balance Sheet	$ -	$ -	$ -
4000-Sales Revenue	Sales	Income Statement	$ -	$ 5,400	-$ 5,400
4100-Cost of Sales	Cost of Sales	Income Statement	$ 4,500	$ -	$ 4,500
4200-Rent Expense	Rent Expense	Income Statement	$ 200	$ -	$ 200
		Total	**$ 16,400**	**$ 16,400**	**$ -**

How Financial Statements are Created from a Trial Balance.

Creating financial statements from a trial balance involves organising and summarising the information to present the financial health and performance of a business.

Start with the Trial Balance:

The trial balance lists all account balances for the period.

Prepare the Income Statement:

List Revenues: Sum all revenue accounts.

List Expenses: Sum all expense accounts.

Calculate Net Profit or Loss: Subtract total expenses from total revenue.

Follow the number references to see how numbers from the trial balance are transferred to the Income Statement.

Financial Statements	
Tees and Giggles Ltd	
Income Statement	Period 1
Date From	01-Jan-27
Date To	31-Jan-27
Sales Revenue	[1] 5,400
Cost of Sales	[2] (4,500)
Gross Profit	**900**
Gross Profit Margin %	**17%**
Expenses	
Wages Expense	0
Wages Oncosts Expense	0
Electricity Expense	0
Rent Expense	[3] (200)
Advertising Expense	0
Subscription Expense	0
Depreciation Expense	0
Total Expenses	**(200)**
Earning Before Interest and Taxation (EBIT)	**700**
EBIT Margin	**13%**
Interest Expense	0
Profit Before Tax (PBT)	**700**
Profit Before Tax Margin	**13%**
Income Tax Expense	**0**
Profit (-Loss) After Tax (PAT)	**700**
Profit (-Loss) After Tax %	**13%**

Trial Balance					
Combined	**Report Row**	**Report**	**Debits**	**Credits**	**Balance**
1000-Cash	Cash	Balance Sheet	$ 11,200	$ -	$ 11,200
1200-T-Shirts	T-Shirts	Balance Sheet	$ 500	$ -	$ 500
1210-Accounts Receivable	Accounts Receivable	Balance Sheet	$ -	$ -	$ -
2100-Accounts Payable	Accounts Payable	Balance Sheet	$ -	$ -	$ -
2500-Bank Loans	Bank Loans	Balance Sheet	$ -	$ 1,000	-$ 1,000
3000-Share Capital	Share Capital	Balance Sheet	$ -	$ 10,000	-$ 10,000
3100-Retained Earnings	Retained Earnings	Balance Sheet	$ -	$ -	$ -
4000-Sales Revenue	Sales Revenue	Income Statement	$ -	$ 5,400	-$ [1] 5,400
4100-Cost of Sales	Cost of Sales	Income Statement	$ 4,500	$ -	$ [2] 4,500
4200-Rent Expense	Rent Expense	Income Statement	$ 200	$ -	$ [3] 200
		Total	**$ 16,400**	**$ 16,400**	**$ -**

Prepare the Balance Sheet:

List Assets: Include all asset accounts.

List Liabilitics: Includc all liability accounts.

Calculate Equity: Include owner's equity and adjust for net profit or loss from the income statement.

Follow the number references to see how numbers from the trial balance are transferred to the balance sheet.

Tees and Giggles Ltd	
Balance Sheet	Period 1
As At	31-Jan-27
Assets	
Current Assets	
Cash	(1) 11,200
Inventory/Stock	(2) 500
Accounts Receivable	0
Prepaid Expenses	0
Total Current Assets	**11,700**
Fixed Assets	
Fixed Assets	0
Accumulated Depreciation	0
Total Fixed Assets	**0**
Total Assets	**11,700**
Current Liabilities	
Accounts Payable	0
Deferred Revenue	0
Accrued Employee Costs	0
Provision for Income Tax	0
Total Current Liabilities	**0**
Long Term Liabilities	
Bank Loans	(3) (1,000)
Total Liabilities	**(1,000)**
Net Assets	**10,700**
Equity	
Share Capital	(4) 10,000
Retained Earnings b/f	0
Retained Earnings	700 (5)
Total Equity	**10,700**

Trial Balance

Combined	Report Row	Report	Debits	Credits	Balance
1000-Cash	Cash	Balance Sheet	$ 11,200	$ -	(1) 11,200
1200-T-Shirts	T-Shirts	Balance Sheet	$ 500	$ -	$ (2) 500
1210-Accounts Receivable	Accounts Receivable	Balance Sheet	$ -	$ -	$ -
2100-Accounts Payable	Accounts Payable	Balance Sheet	$ -	$ -	$ -
2500-Bank Loans	Bank Loans	Balance Sheet	$ -	$ 1,000	-$ (3) 1,000
3000-Share Capital	Share Capital	Balance Sheet	$ -	$ 10,000	-$ (4) 10,000
3100-Retained Earnings	Retained Earnings	Balance Sheet	$ -	$ -	$ -
4000-Sales Revenue	Sales Revenue	Income Statement	$ -	$ 5,400	-$ 5,400
4100-Cost of Sales	Cost of Sales	Income Statement	$ 4,500	$ (5)	$ 4,500
4200-Rent Expense	Rent Expense	Income Statement	$ 200	$ -	$ 200
		Total	**$ 16,400**	**$ 16,400**	**$ -**

Retained earnings is the Net Profit.

Sales Revenue: $5,400

Less:
Cost of Sales: - $4,500
Rent Expense - $200

Net Profit - $700

(5)

Prepare the Cash Flow Statement:

Operating Activities: Classify operating activities. These are normal trading activities.

Investing Activities: Record cash spent on or received from buying or selling assets.

Financing Activities: Record cash from loans or investments and repayments.

Follow the number references to see how the cash flow analysis is transferred to the cash flow statement.

Tees and Giggles Ltd		
Statement of Cash Flows	**Period 1**	
Date From	01-Jan-27	
Date To	31-Jan-27	
Operating Cash		
Receipts from Customers	5,400	1
Payments to Staff	0	
Payments to Suppliers	(5,200)	2, 3
Loan Interest Payment	0	
Income Taxes Paid	0	
Net Operating Cash	**200**	
Investing		
Payments for Fixed Assets	0	
Financing		
Cash from Shareholders	10,000	4
Dividend Paid	0	
Bank Loans Received	1,000	5
Loan Principle Repayments	0	
Net Cash for The Period	**11,200**	
Opening Cash	0	
Closing Cash	**11,200**	

Coding Transactions in The Ledger

Transaction No.		1		
Date		1/01/2027		
Transfer cash from personal account to the business account.				
Account & Description		**Amount**	**Report**	**Cash Analysis**
1000-Cash	$	4 → 10,000	Balance Sheet	Cash from Owner
3000-Share Capital	-$	10,000	Balance Sheet	

Transaction No.		2		
Date		1/01/2027		
Borrow money from the bank.				
Account		**Amount**	**Report Row Description**	**Cash Analysis**
1000-Cash	$	5 → 1,000	Balance Sheet	Cash from Loans
2500-Bank Loans	-$	1,000	Balance Sheet	

Transaction No.		3		
Date		1/01/2027		
Purchase T-shirts				
Account		**Amount**	**Report Row Description**	**Cash Analysis**
1200-T-Shirts	$	5,000	Balance Sheet	
2100-Accounts Payable	-$	5,000	Balance Sheet	
2100-Accounts Payable	$	5,000	Balance Sheet	
1000-Cash	-$	2 → 5,000	Balance Sheet	Cash Spent on Stock

Transaction No.		4		
Date		1/01/2027		
Sell T-shirts				
Account		**Amount**	**Report Row Description**	**Cash Analysis**
1210-Accounts Receivable	$	5,400	Balance Sheet	
4000-Sales Revenue	-$	5,400	Income Statement	
1000-Cash	$	1 → 5,400	Balance Sheet	Cash Received from Sales
1210-Accounts Receivable	-$	5,400	Balance Sheet	
4100-Cost of Sales	$	4,500	Income Statement	
1200-T-Shirts	-$	4,500	Balance Sheet	

Transaction No.		5		
Date		1/01/2027		
Pay rent for the month				
Account		**Amount**	**Report Row Description**	**Cash Analysis**
4200-Rent Expense	$	200	Income Statement	
2100-Accounts Payable	-$	200	Balance Sheet	
2100-Accounts Payable	$	200	Balance Sheet	
1000-Cash	-$	3 → 200	Balance Sheet	Cash Spent on Rent

Business Performance Assessment using Financial Statements.

The financial statements presented are for a T-shirt business from January 1, 2027, to January 31, 2027. Let's break down each statement and understand what it tells us about the business.

In summary, the business has returned a profit of $700 (13% profit margin) compared with the return from the bank deposit of $36.67 (.37% profit margin).

Income Statement

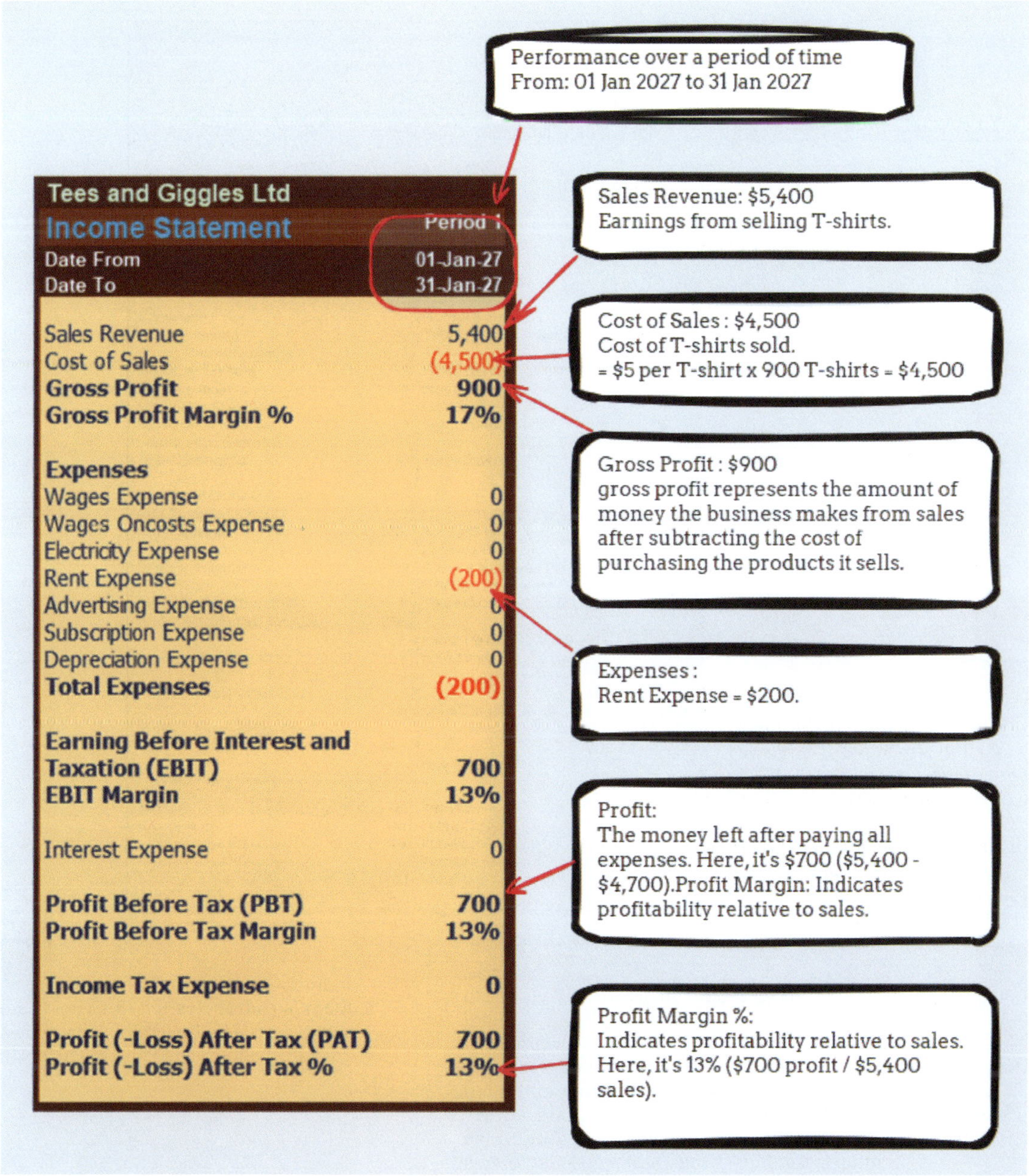

Balance Sheet

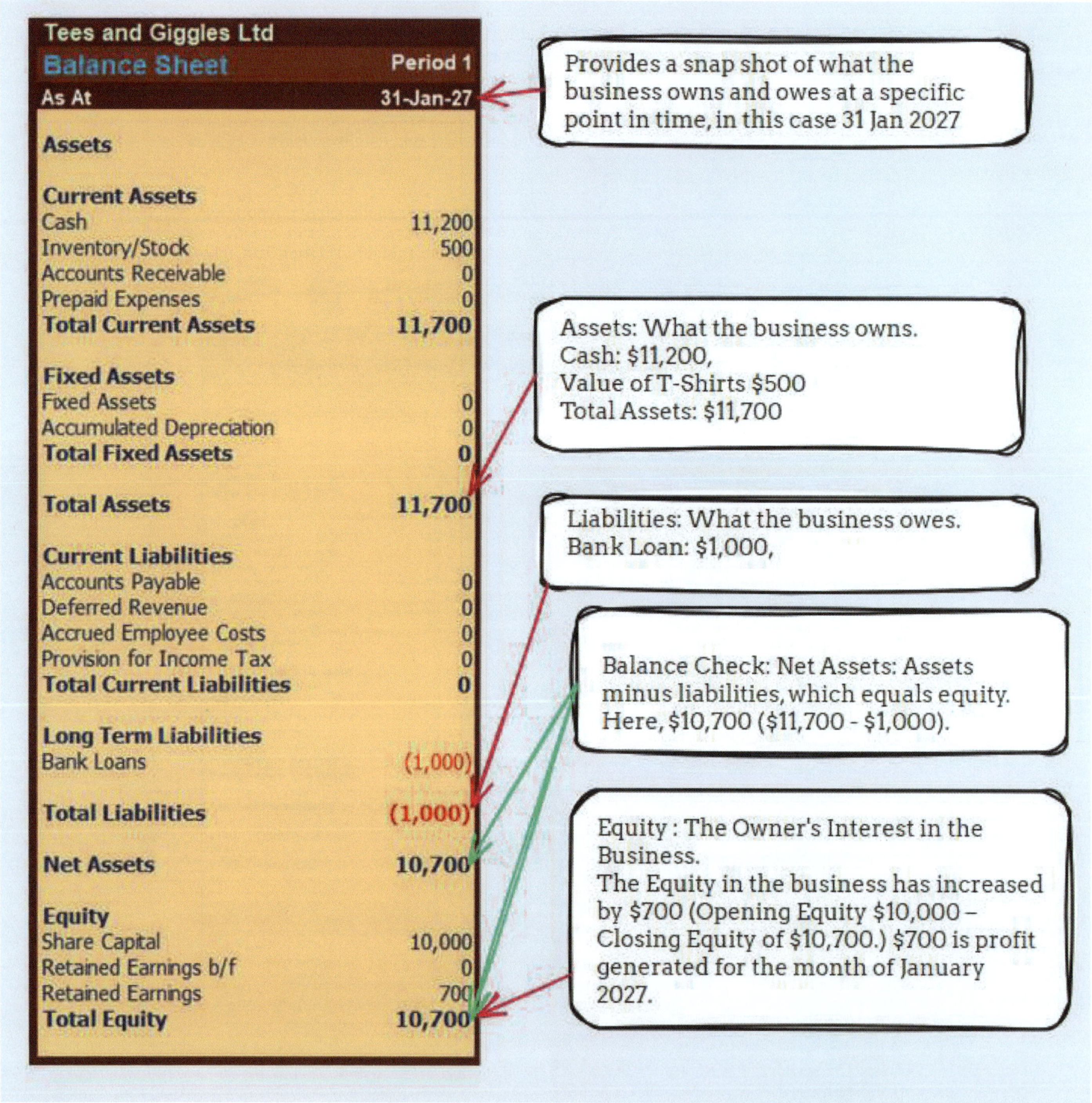

Tees and Giggles Ltd	
Balance Sheet	Period 1
As At	31-Jan-27
Assets	
Current Assets	
Cash	11,200
Inventory/Stock	500
Accounts Receivable	0
Prepaid Expenses	0
Total Current Assets	**11,700**
Fixed Assets	
Fixed Assets	0
Accumulated Depreciation	0
Total Fixed Assets	**0**
Total Assets	**11,700**
Current Liabilities	
Accounts Payable	0
Deferred Revenue	0
Accrued Employee Costs	0
Provision for Income Tax	0
Total Current Liabilities	**0**
Long Term Liabilities	
Bank Loans	(1,000)
Total Liabilities	**(1,000)**
Net Assets	**10,700**
Equity	
Share Capital	10,000
Retained Earnings b/f	0
Retained Earnings	700
Total Equity	**10,700**

Cash Flow Statement

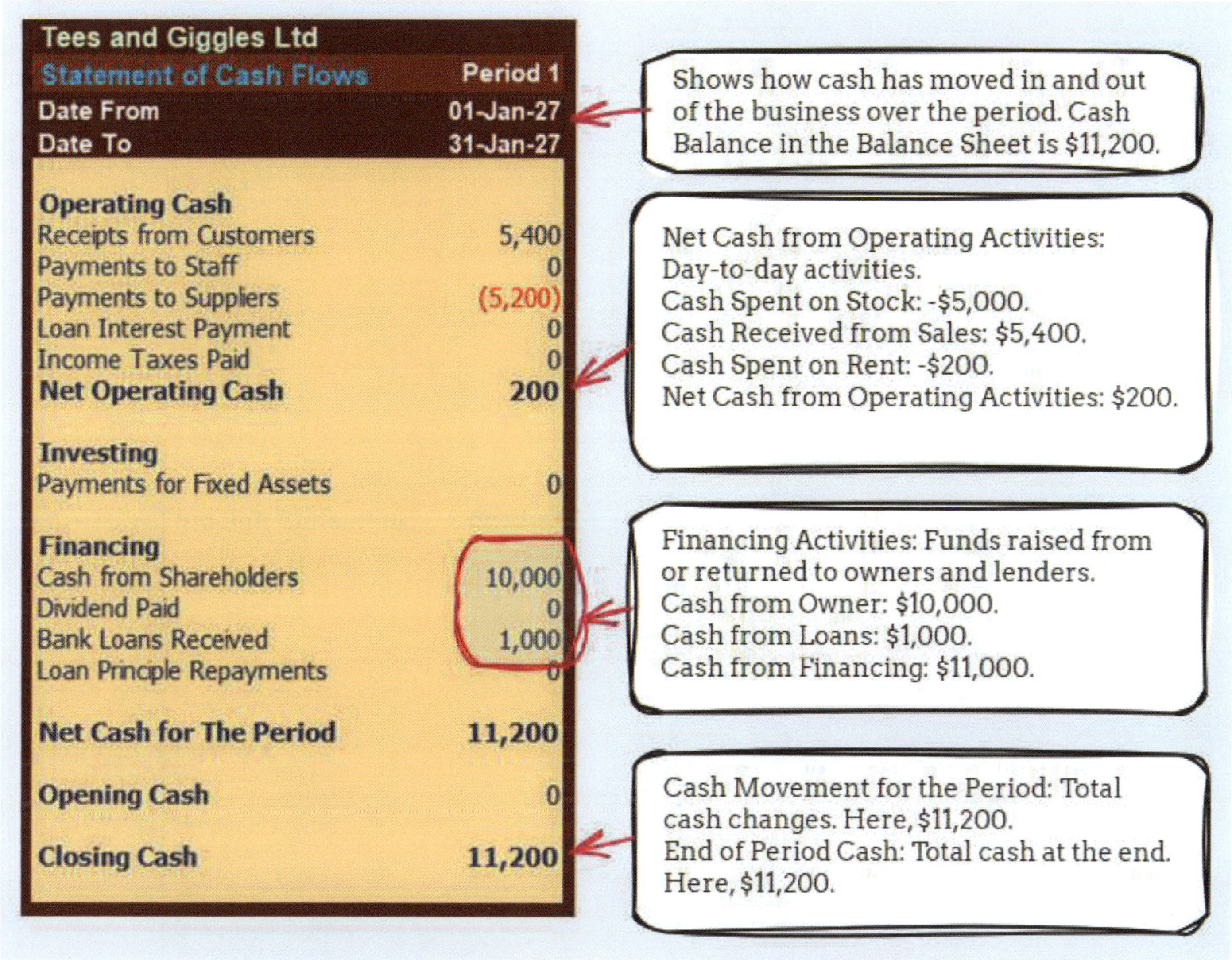

Tees and Giggles Ltd	
Statement of Cash Flows	**Period 1**
Date From	01-Jan-27
Date To	31-Jan-27
Operating Cash	
Receipts from Customers	5,400
Payments to Staff	0
Payments to Suppliers	(5,200)
Loan Interest Payment	0
Income Taxes Paid	0
Net Operating Cash	**200**
Investing	
Payments for Fixed Assets	0
Financing	
Cash from Shareholders	10,000
Dividend Paid	0
Bank Loans Received	1,000
Loan Principle Repayments	0
Net Cash for The Period	**11,200**
Opening Cash	0
Closing Cash	**11,200**

Summary showing the three main reports side by side.

Now that you understand how business events are categorised and summarised into financial statements. In modern businesses, thousands of transactions are processed, and reports are generated using sophisticated accounting software. Below is a recap of how each main report relates to the other.

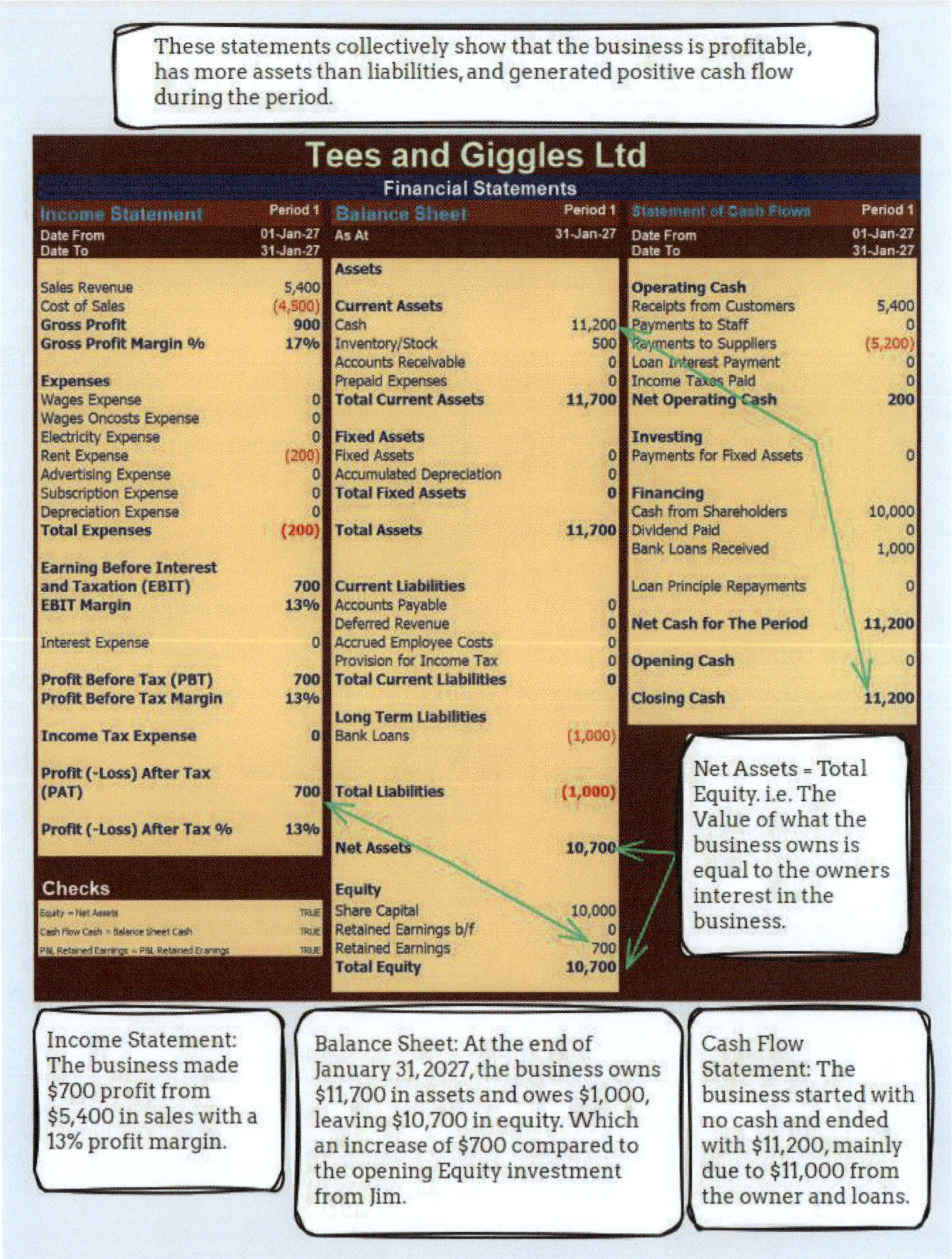

These statements collectively show that the business is profitable, has more assets than liabilities, and generated positive cash flow during the period.

Tees and Giggles Ltd

Financial Statements

Income Statement	Period 1
Date From	01-Jan-27
Date To	31-Jan-27
Sales Revenue	5,400
Cost of Sales	(4,500)
Gross Profit	**900**
Gross Profit Margin %	**17%**
Expenses	
Wages Expense	0
Wages Oncosts Expense	0
Electricity Expense	0
Rent Expense	(200)
Advertising Expense	0
Subscription Expense	0
Depreciation Expense	0
Total Expenses	**(200)**
Earning Before Interest and Taxation (EBIT)	**700**
EBIT Margin	**13%**
Interest Expense	0
Profit Before Tax (PBT)	**700**
Profit Before Tax Margin	**13%**
Income Tax Expense	**0**
Profit (-Loss) After Tax (PAT)	**700**
Profit (-Loss) After Tax %	**13%**

Checks	
Equity = Net Assets	TRUE
Cash Flow Cash = Balance Sheet Cash	TRUE
P&L Retained Earnings = P&L Retained Eranings	TRUE

Balance Sheet	Period 1
As At	31-Jan-27
Assets	
Current Assets	
Cash	11,200
Inventory/Stock	500
Accounts Receivable	0
Prepaid Expenses	0
Total Current Assets	**11,700**
Fixed Assets	
Fixed Assets	0
Accumulated Depreciation	0
Total Fixed Assets	**0**
Total Assets	**11,700**
Current Liabilities	
Accounts Payable	0
Deferred Revenue	0
Accrued Employee Costs	0
Provision for Income Tax	0
Total Current Liabilities	**0**
Long Term Liabilities	
Bank Loans	(1,000)
Total Liabilities	**(1,000)**
Net Assets	**10,700**
Equity	
Share Capital	10,000
Retained Earnings b/f	0
Retained Earnings	700
Total Equity	**10,700**

Statement of Cash Flows	Period 1
Date From	01-Jan-27
Date To	31-Jan-27
Operating Cash	
Receipts from Customers	5,400
Payments to Staff	0
Payments to Suppliers	(5,200)
Loan Interest Payment	0
Income Taxes Paid	0
Net Operating Cash	**200**
Investing	
Payments for Fixed Assets	0
Financing	
Cash from Shareholders	10,000
Dividend Paid	0
Bank Loans Received	1,000
Loan Principle Repayments	0
Net Cash for The Period	**11,200**
Opening Cash	**0**
Closing Cash	**11,200**

Net Assets = Total Equity. i.e. The Value of what the business owns is equal to the owners interest in the business.

Income Statement: The business made $700 profit from $5,400 in sales with a 13% profit margin.

Balance Sheet: At the end of January 31, 2027, the business owns $11,700 in assets and owes $1,000, leaving $10,700 in equity. Which an increase of $700 compared to the opening Equity investment from Jim.

Cash Flow Statement: The business started with no cash and ended with $11,200, mainly due to $11,000 from the owner and loans.

Chapter 04: Skill-Building Exercises and Questions

Task 1: Do you have access to your business's or your Employer's Chart of Accounts? If not, please ask your Accountant or your Accounting Team for a copy.

If the business receives an invoice for stationery from the supplier, what code will be allocated to items purchased?

Code Number:

Task 2: Use the accounting simulator online application to answer the following questions. The Simulator can be accessed using the link below and update the numbers in the "Five Events" Section - "Dark Blue" Cells are input cells.

Use the link below to answer the following question.

https://magicofaccounting.ecoachinghub.com/exercises

Markup on Cost = 30%

Cost of T-shirts = $3

Income Tax % = 30%

How will the below changes in inputs impact the original reported numbers?

Total Revenue

Net Profit After Tax

Total Assets

Total Liabilities

Net Assets

Net Operating Cash

Closing Cash Balance

How to use the Accounting Simulator.

Log into:

https://magicofaccounting.ecoachinghub.com/exercises

Chapter 4 Exercise

Go to the "Five Events Tab in the simulator below and change the following inputs:

Markup on Cost = 30% (In Book = 20%)

Cost of T-shirts = $3 (In Book = $5)

Income Tax % = 30% (In Book = 0%)

Record The Following Numbers from The Financial Statements:
Net Profit After Tax. (In Book = $700)
Total Assets. (In Book = $11,700)
Total Liabilities. (In Book = $1,000)
Net Assets. (In Book = $10,700)
Net Operating Cash. (In Book = $200)
Closing Cash Balance. (In Book $11,200)

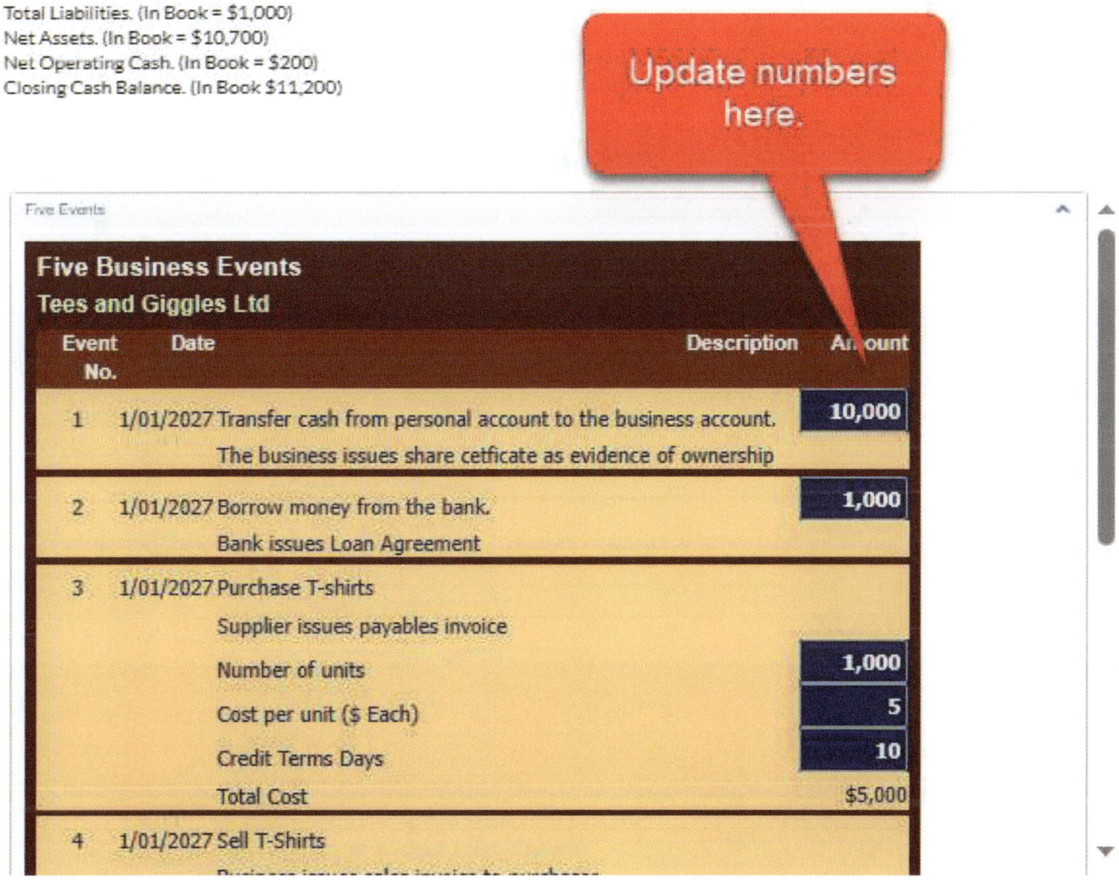

Chapter 4 Exercise

Go to the "Five Events Tab in the simulator below and change the following inputs:

Markup on Cost = 30% (In Book = 20%)

Cost of T-shirts = $3 (In Book = $5)

Income Tax % = 30% (In Book = 0%)

Record The Following Numbers from The Financial Statements:
Net Profit After Tax. (In Book = $700)
Total Assets. (In Book = $11,700)
Total Liabilities. (In Book = $1,000)
Net Assets. (In Book = $10,700)
Net Operating Cash. (In Book = $200)
Closing Cash Balance. (In Book $11,200)

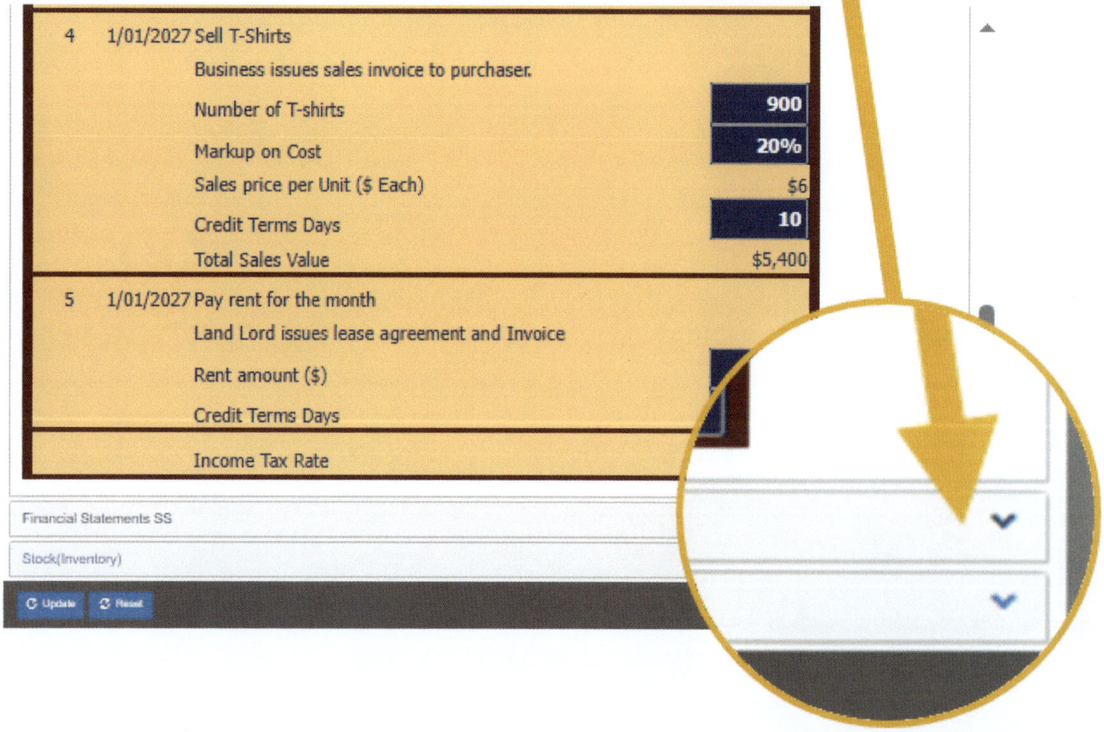

Well done! You learned about the process of producing financial statements, including the steps of recording, classifying, and summarizing financial transactions.

Part 2 - The Accounting Profession and Rules of Accounting

Now that you've dipped your toes into the basics, it's time to dive deeper into the professional world of accounting. In this part, you'll explore the rigorous standards and ethical guidelines that ensure the trustworthiness of financial reports. You'll meet the key players in the world of accounting, like standard setters and professional bodies, and understand how audits and record-keeping maintain the integrity of financial Information. This part also brings accounting concepts to life with real-world applications of GAAP and IFRS, showing how these rules transform raw data into meaningful insights.

Chapter 05: Accounting Integrity

Chapter 05 Objective: Comprehend the role of accounting standards, professional bodies, and audits in maintaining the integrity and reliability of financial statements.

Before we discuss Cash vs Accruals Accounting and specific adjusting entries such as accruals, deferrals, depreciation, and amortisation (this is where the magic happens!), it's important to understand the regulatory framework that governs these adjustments.

The accounting profession ensures trustworthy accounting by establishing rigorous standards, adherence to ethical guidelines, continuous education, stringent regulatory oversight, and auditing processes. Here's how this process is structured and the roles played by standard setters, professional accounting bodies, and auditors:

Role of Standard Setters

Standard setters are organisations responsible for developing and issuing accounting standards that provide a framework for consistent and transparent financial reporting.

Financial Accounting Standards Board (FASB):

Function: Develops and issues Generally Accepted Accounting Principles (GAAP) in the United States, ensuring that financial statements are accurate, consistent, and comparable.

Source: FASB

International Accounting Standards Board (IASB):

Function: Issues International Financial Reporting Standards (IFRS), which are used globally to ensure uniformity in financial reporting across different jurisdictions.

Source: IASB

Role of Professional Accounting Bodies

Professional accounting bodies oversee the certification, education, and ethical standards of accountants. They play a crucial role in maintaining the integrity and competence of the profession.

See the Appendix 2, found in Part 4, for a detailed list of professional accounting bodies and their websites.

If your accountant is a member of one of these organisations, you can be confident that they are well-trained to provide information that complies with the required accounting standards.

Accounting Policies Chosen by Organisations

While GAAP and IFRS provide broad guidelines, individual organisations choose specific accounting policies that best suit their operations, industry and locations.

Key Points:

Accounting policies are the specific principles and procedures a company uses to prepare its financial statements.

Companies must disclose their chosen accounting policies in their financial reports.

Consistency in accounting policies helps in comparing financial performance over time.

Examples include - Depreciation Policy, Inventory/Stock valuation policy etc.

How you can help your accounting team, Accountant, Tax agent?

Supporting your accounting team and external advisors can improve the efficiency and accuracy of financial reporting.

Key Points:

Provide timely and complete information about financial transactions.

Remember to keep organized records and documentation. Accountants and tax agents are highly paid professionals. Keep your records in order and make a list with explanations. It's not a good use of your money to pay these professionals to do this administrative work.

Communicate openly about business operations and changes.

Be proactive in understanding the basics of financial reporting and compliance.

Chapter 05: Skill-Building Exercises and Questions

Exercise 1: Reviewing Accounting Policies

Identify one accounting policy that your business or a business you know follows. Explain why this policy might be important for the business.

Exercise 2: Write down three ways you can help your accounting team or accountant in their work. Discuss how these actions can improve financial reporting.

Well done! You understood the importance of accounting standards, professional bodies, and audits in maintaining the integrity and reliability of financial reporting.

Audits

An audit is an independent examination of financial statements by a qualified professional (auditor) to assure the users of Financial Statements that they are free from material misstatement. Not all entities require an audit - these are confined to specific companies under legislature direction.

Key Points:

Audits enhance the credibility of financial statements.

They help detect and prevent fraud and errors.

Auditors provide an opinion on whether the financial statements comply with relevant accounting standards.

Record Keeping and Evidence

Accurate record-keeping is the foundation of reliable financial reporting. Good record-keeping involves maintaining detailed and organised documentation of all financial transactions. This also makes accounting records one of the most reliable records of information about an organisation.

Key Points:

Essential for preparing accurate financial statements.

Supports compliance with legal and regulatory requirements.

Helps in the event of audits and reviews by providing evidence of transactions.

In accounting, there are various types of documents that are essential for record-keeping and financial transparency. These include primary source documents like invoices, receipts, and purchase orders, as well as books of original entry such as the general journal, sales journal, and purchase journal. Subsidiary ledgers like the accounts receivable ledger and inventory ledger provide detailed records supporting the amounts reported in the general ledger. Supporting schedules, reconciliation documents, internal reports, external reports, contracts, electronic records, and audit trails also play important roles in maintaining accurate financial records and complying with regulatory requirements.

Chapter 06: Accounting Concepts and Standards

Chapter 06 Objective: Explore fundamental accounting concepts and standards, such as GAAP and IFRS, and understand their application in financial reporting.

Role of Accounting Concepts and Accounting Standards.

Accounting concepts are fundamental principles that guide the accounting process, ensuring consistency and reliability. Accounting standards, like **IFRS** (International Financial Reporting Standards) and **GAAP** (Generally Accepted Accounting Principles), provide detailed rules and guidelines for financial reporting. Adjusting entries are changes made in the accounting records at the end of an accounting period to ensure that revenues and expenses are recorded in the in accordance with GAAP and Accounting Standards correctly in the correct period. Here's how these concepts relate to each other and require adjusting entries, explained with examples for Tees and Giggles Ltd.

If you pay closer attention to the concepts below, you will realise that they are logical and based on common sense.

Entity Concept

Definition: The business is treated as a separate entity distinct from its owner(s). Financial transactions of the business are recorded separately from the personal transactions of the owner(s).

Example: If Jim uses personal funds to buy a car for personal use. These transactions are not recorded in the company's books.

Money Measurement Concept

Definition: Only transactions that can be measured in monetary terms are recorded in the accounting records.

Example: Employee morale or customer satisfaction is not recorded; only the sales revenue from T-shirts sold is.

Going Concern Concept

Definition: It is assumed that the business will continue to operate indefinitely unless there is evidence to suggest otherwise.

Example: The T-shirt business values its inventory based on the assumption it will continue to sell T-shirts. If it was assumed not to continue, the stock will be valued at scrap value.

Cost Concept

Definition: Assets are recorded at their original purchase cost, not at their current market value.

Example: A T-shirt printing machine bought for $5,000 is recorded at $5,000, even if its market value changes.

Dual Aspect or Duality Concept

Definition: Every financial transaction affects at least two accounts, ensuring the accounting equation (Assets = Liabilities + Equity) remains balanced.

Example: Selling T-shirts for $25,000 increases Accounts Receivable (asset) by $25,000 and sales revenue by $25,000 (equity/(retained earnings)).

Matching Concept

The matching concept is a fundamental accounting principle that requires expenses to be recorded in the same period as the revenues they help generate. This ensures that the income statement reflects the true profitability of a business within a specific period. Here's how this concept applies to Cost of Goods Sold (COGS), Depreciation, and Prepayments, explained with examples for a retail T-shirt business.

Definition: The matching concept states that expenses should be recorded in the same period as the revenues they help generate. This ensures that the financial statements present a fair and accurate view of the company's financial performance.

Example 1: Cost of Goods Sold (COGS)

Scenario: Imagine a retail T-shirt business that purchases 1,000 T-shirts (Inventory/Stock) on 15/01/2027 for $5,000 therefore the cost for each T-shit is $5.

The cost is initially recorded as inventory (an asset). The corresponding entry is Accounts Payable. Recognising liability for paying the T-shirt supplier.

The 1000 T-shirts held in stock are sold on 16/01/2027 for $25,000. The $25,000 is recognised as Sales Revenue. According to the matching concept, the cost of the T-shirts sold are matched with the sales revenue to show the true profitability. i.e.

Sales Revenue = $25,000

Cost of Sales = $5,000 (Value of T-shirts sold)

Profit = $20,000 ($25,000 Less $5,000)

Example 2: Depreciation

Depreciation Explained: Depreciation is the systematic allocation of the cost of a tangible asset over its useful life. It reflects the usage and wear and tear of the asset.

Scenario: Consider the same T-shirt business that purchases a T-shirt printing machine for $5,000. The machine has an expected useful life of 3 years.

Application of the Matching Concept:

The printing machine is purchased and recorded as an asset.

Entry: Increase in Printing Machine (Asset) $5,000, Increase in Accounts Payable $5,000.

Depreciation Calculation:

Annual Depreciation Expense: $5,000 / 3 years (36 months) = $139 per month.

Recording Depreciation:

Each month, $139 is recorded as a depreciation expense to match the cost of the machine with the revenues it helps generate over its useful life.

Entry: Increase Depreciation Expense $139, Increase Accumulated Depreciation $139.

Example 3: Prepayments

Prepayments Explained: Prepayments are payments made in advance for goods or services to be received in the future. These are initially recorded as assets and expensed over the period they relate to.

Scenario: The T-shirt business purchases a 12-month subscription for accounting software for $24,000 on 3/01/2027.

The $24,000 payment covers 12 months of service, so each month's expense is $2,000.

Initially, the payment is recorded as a prepaid expense (an asset).

Recording the Transaction:

Initial Payment:

Entry: Increase Prepaid Expenses Asset $24,000, Increase Accounts Payable Liability $24,000, recognising a payment due to in the future to the asset supplier.

Monthly Expense Recognition:

Each month, $2,000 is expensed to match the cost with the period it helps generate revenue.

Entry: Increase Software Expense $2,000, Reduce Prepaid Expenses Asset $2,000.

Conservatism Concept

Definition: Accountants should choose the option that least likely overstates assets and income.

Example: If there's uncertainty about collecting an account receivable, record a provision for doubtful accounts.

Adjusting Entry: Record an allowance for doubtful accounts.

Materiality Concept

Definition: All significant information that could influence the decision-making process of users should be recorded and reported.

Example: A small expense like buying office supplies might not be significant, but large expenses like purchasing a new printing machine should be recorded.

Related Standard: IFRS requires that significant transactions must be disclosed in financial statements.

Adjusting Entry: Ensure all material transactions are recorded.

Objectivity Concept

Definition: Financial information should be based on verifiable evidence and free from bias.

6. Share Certificates

Examples of documents used as evidence before recording transactions are: Purchase invoices, Sales Invoices, Payroll Records, Bank Statements, Loan Agreements, Share Certificates, Accounting Policies and Adjusting Entires Approved by Authorised Person and Supporting Documentation.

Example: Sales of T-shirts should be supported by verifiable source documents.

Accrual Concept

Definition: Transactions are recorded when they occur, not only when cash is exchanged. This means recognising revenues when earned and expenses when incurred, regardless of cash flow.

Example: At year-end, if the business delivered T-shirts worth $500 but hasn't received payment yet:

Entry: Increase Accounts Receivable by $500, Increase Sales Revenue by $500.

Consistency Concept

Definition: The same accounting principles and methods should be used from period to period. This consistency helps in comparing financial statements over time.

Example: If using straight-line depreciation for the printing machine, continue to use it in subsequent periods.

Related Standard: IFRS requires consistent application of accounting methods.

Adjusting Entry: No specific adjusting entry, but review for consistency.

Prudence Concept

Definition: Accounting should be conservative and prudent. Revenues and profits should only be recognised when they are reasonably certain, while expenses and losses should be recognised as soon as they are known.

Example: Do not record anticipated sales until they occur.

Related Standard: IFRS encourages conservatism.

Adjusting Entry: Ensure potential losses are recorded promptly, but gains are only recognised when certain.

Full Disclosure Concept

Definition: All relevant financial information should be disclosed in the financial statements. This includes any facts that would influence the judgment of an informed user.

Example: Include notes on any pending lawsuits or significant transactions.

Related Standard: IFRS requires full disclosure in financial statements.

Adjusting Entry: Ensure all relevant information is included in the notes to the financial statements.

Accruals Basis Accounting vs Cash Basis Accounting

Cash vs. Accrual Accounting Explained

Cash Accounting

Definition: Cash accounting is a simple accounting method where revenues and expenses are recorded only when cash is received or paid. Only small businesses are allowed to use Cash Accounting, with some other exceptions like farming businesses.

How It Works:

Revenue: Recorded when cash is received, regardless of when the sale was made.

Expenses: Recorded when cash is paid out, regardless of when the expense was incurred.

Example:

If a T-shirt business sells a shirt in December but receives payment in January, the revenue is recorded in January.

Similarly, if the business buys inventory in November but pays the supplier in December, the expense is recorded in December.

Advantages:

Simplicity: Easy to understand and implement.

Immediate Cash Flow Tracking: Provides a clear picture of cash on hand.

Disadvantages:

Misleading Financial Health: Doesn't show money that is owed or expected, leading to a distorted view of profitability and financial health.

Accrual Accounting

Definition: Accrual accounting records revenues and expenses when they are earned or incurred, regardless of when cash is exchanged. The accrual accounting method is often mandated and preferred by larger businesses and those required to adhere to international accounting standards, such as the International Financial Reporting Standards (IFRS) and Generally Accepted Accounting Principles (GAAP).

How It Works:

Revenue: Recorded when earned, even if payment hasn't been received yet.

Expenses: Recorded when incurred, even if payment hasn't been made yet.

Example:

If a T-shirt business sells a shirt in December and receives payment in January, the revenue is still recorded in December.

If the business buys inventory in November but pays the supplier in December, the expense is recorded in November.

Advantages:

Accurate Financial Picture: Reflects the true financial position by including all earned revenues and incurred expenses.

Better Matching of Revenues and Expenses: Ensures that income statements accurately reflect profitability by matching revenues with related expenses within the same period.

Improved Decision-Making: Provides more reliable financial information for planning and decision-making.

Disadvantages:

Complexity: More complicated to implement and maintain.

Non-Cash Realities: May show profits when there is no cash flow, which requires careful cash management.

Why Accrual Accounting is Preferable

1. True Financial Health:

Accurate Picture: Accrual accounting provides a more accurate picture of a business's financial health by including all earned revenues and incurred expenses, not just cash transactions. This helps businesses understand their actual profitability and financial position.

Example: If your T-shirt business makes a big sale in December but receives payment in January, accrual accounting ensures that the revenue is recognised when the sale occurs, providing a true reflection of your business's performance in December.

2. Better Matching Principle:

Revenue and Expense Matching: Accrual accounting matches revenues with the expenses incurred to generate those revenues within the same period. This principle ensures that financial statements accurately reflect business operations.

Example: If you purchase materials to make T-shirts in November and sell them in December, accrual accounting records the expenses in November and the revenue in December, matching them correctly to show true profitability.

3. Improved Financial Planning:

Informed Decisions: With a complete picture of cash and credit transactions, businesses can make better-informed financial decisions, plan for the future, and manage their operations more effectively.

Example: Knowing that you have upcoming receivables and payables helps in planning for inventory purchases, marketing campaigns, and other business activities.

4. Compliance and Professional Standards:

Regulatory Requirements: Many financial reporting standards, including IFRS and GAAP, require accrual accounting for publicly traded companies and larger businesses. This method ensures compliance with these regulations and enhances credibility with investors and stakeholders.

Example: If you plan to expand your T-shirt business or seek investors, using accrual accounting can make your financial statements more credible and professional.

5. Long-Term Business Growth:

Sustainability: Accrual accounting supports sustainable business growth by providing a clear and consistent financial framework. This approach helps in tracking long-term performance and financial trends.

Example: As your T-shirt business grows, accurate financial data helps secure loans, attract investors, and make strategic decisions that support continued expansion.

Conclusion

While cash accounting is simpler and provides an immediate view of cash flow, accrual accounting offers a more comprehensive and accurate picture of a business's financial health. By recognising revenues and expenses when they are earned or incurred, accrual accounting ensures that financial statements reflect the business's true performance, facilitating better decision-making and long-term growth. For these reasons, accrual accounting is generally preferred and often required by accounting standards like IFRS and GAAP.

Multiple Choice Questions for Chapter 6: Accounting Concepts and Standards, Answers and Explanations are in Appendix 4.

---

1. Which accounting concept ensures that a business will continue to operate indefinitely unless there is evidence to suggest otherwise?

A. Cost Concept

B. Going Concern Concept

C. Money Measurement Concept

D. Dual Aspect Concept

---

2. According to the Matching Concept, expenses should be recorded:

A. When cash is paid out

B. In the same period as the revenues they help generate

C. When the invoice is received

D. At the end of the financial year

---

3. Which concept states that only transactions that can be measured in monetary terms are recorded in the accounting records?

A. Entity Concept

B. Money Measurement Concept

C. Going Concern Concept

D. Dual Aspect Concept

---

4. The principle that expenses and losses should be recognized as soon as they are known, while revenues and profits should only be recognized when they are reasonably certain is known as:

A. Conservatism Concept

B. Consistency Concept

C. Prudence Concept

D. Full Disclosure Concept

---

5. Which concept requires that financial transactions of the business are recorded separately from the personal transactions of the owner(s)?

A. Dual Aspect Concept

B. Entity Concept

C. Materiality Concep

D. Objectivity Concep

Well done! You explored fundamental accounting concepts and standards, such as GAAP and IFRS, and their practical application in financial reporting.

Chapter 07: Practical Example of GAAP and IFRS in Action.

Chapter 07 Objective: Demonstrate the practical application of GAAP and IFRS through a detailed example, illustrating how accounting adjustments and financial statements are produced. Financial statement layouts are repeated deliberately to familiarise you with the layout of Financial Statements.

This chapter aims to consolidate what you have learned so far using a business scenario to demonstrate accrual accounting, including the standard accounting adjustments used to accurately show a business's financial status in compliance with GAAP and IFRS.

We will assume that Tees and Giggles Ltd is required to use Accrual accounting.

Recapping: Accrual Accounting records revenues and expenses when they are earned or incurred, regardless of when the cash is exchanged.

Some transactions are adjusted to comply with accounting concepts and accounting standards, we will discuss these in detail as we go through the business events.

These adjustments are:

1. Cost of Goods Sold Adjustment

2. Deferred Sales Adjustment

3. Depreciation Adjustment

4. Prepayment expense adjustment

5. Accrued Expenses Adjustment

We won't delve into the accounting process in detail as it was covered in Chapter 04.

List of Events in this example.

Accounting identifies, classifies, summarises, and reports transactions arising from business events.

We will explore these transactions in the Tees and Giggles Ltd business and how they are reflected in the Financial Statements.

In this example, we assume that no GST or Sales Taxes are applicable to any transactions.

List of Events

No	Day-to-day Language Description	Date	Amount	Adjusting Entry (Yes/No)
1.0	The owner invests money into the business.	1/01/2027	$21,000	No
2.1	The business receives a loan from the bank.	2/01/2027	$10,000	No
2.2	The business repays first loan repayment.	31/01/2027	$439	No
2.3	Interest on the loan.	31/01/2027	$42	No
2.4	Repays part of the loan principal.	31/01/2027	$397	No
3.1	The business buys inventory (Invoice received).	15/01/2027	$5,000	No
3.2	The business pays the inventory supplier.	25/01/2027	$5,000	No
4.1	The business Invoices Customer for T-Shirs Sold.	16/01/2027	$25,000	No
4.2	Revenue is deferred for accounting purposes.	31/01/2027	$5,000	Yes
4.3	The business receives payments from customers.	26/01/2027	$25,000	No
4.4	The cost of goods sold is recognised.	31/01/2027	$4,000	Yes
5.1	The business buys fixed assets (Invoice Received).	3/01/2027	$5,000	No
5.2	The business pays the Fixed Asset supplier.	13/01/2027	$5,000	No
5.3	Depreciation is recorded on fixed assets.	31/01/2027	$139	Yes
6.1	The business buys software subscription (invoice received).	3/01/2027	$24,000	No
6.2	The business pays the software supplier.	13/01/2027	$24,000	No
6.3	The prepaid subscription expense is recognised.	31/01/2027	$2,000	Yes
7.1	The business pays salaries and wages expenses.	3/01/2027	$5,000	No
7.2	Accrued on costs for salaries are recorded.	31/01/2027	$1,000	Yes
7.3	The business pays accrued on costs for salaries.	13/01/2027	$1,000	No
8.1	The business receives electricity invoice for the month.	3/01/2027	$1,000	No
8.2	The business pays the electricity supplier.	13/01/2027	$1,000	No
9.1	The business receives advertising invoice for the month.	3/01/2027	$2,000	No
9.2	The business pays the advertising supplier.	13/01/2027	$2,000	No
10.1	The business receives rent invoice.	3/01/2027	$3,000	No
10.2	The business pays rent invoice.	13/01/2027	$3,000	No

Event 01: The Owner Invests Money in the Business.

Event 01: The Owner Invests Money in the Business.

Commercial Purpose

The commercial purpose of the owner's investment of $21,000 into Tees and Giggles Ltd is to provide the business with the necessary capital to fund its operations, purchase inventory, and cover initial expenses. This investment strengthens the financial position of the company by increasing its cash reserves, enabling it to meet short-term obligations and invest in growth opportunities.

Source Documents

Bank Deposit Slip: Evidence of the $21,000 cash deposit into the business bank account.

The owner invests money in the business.

Amount	21,000.00
Date	1/01/2027

Tees and Giggles Ltd

Financial Statements

Income Statement	Period 1
Date From	01-Jan-27
Date To	31-Jan-27
Sales Revenue	0
Cost of Sales	0
Gross Profit	**0**
Gross Profit Margin %	**0%**
Expenses	
Wages Expense	0
Wages Oncosts Expense	0
Electricity Expense	0
Rent Expense	0
Advertising Expense	0
Subscription Expense	0
Depreciation Expense	0
Total Expenses	**0**
Earning Before Interest and Taxation (EBIT)	**0**
EBIT Margin	**0%**
Interest Expense	0
Profit Before Tax (PBT)	**0**
Profit Before Tax Margin	**0%**
Income Tax Expense	**0**
Profit (-Loss) After Tax (PAT)	**0**
Profit (-Loss) After Tax %	**0%**

Checks	
Equity = Net Assets	TRUE
Cash Flow Cash = Balance Sheet Cash	TRUE
P&L Retained Earnings = P&L Retained Eranings	TRUE

Balance Sheet	Period 1
As At	31-Jan-27
Assets	
Current Assets	
Cash	21,000
Inventory/Stock	0
Accounts Receivable	0
Prepaid Expenses	0
Total Current Assets	**21,000**
Fixed Assets	
Fixed Assets	0
Accumulated Depreciation	0
Total Fixed Assets	**0**
Total Assets	**21,000**
Current Liabilities	
Accounts Payable	0
Deferred Revenue	0
Accrued Employee Costs	0
Provision for Income Tax	0
Total Current Liabilities	**0**
Long Term Liabilities	
Bank Loans	0
Total Liabilities	**0**
Net Assets	**21,000**
Equity	
Share Capital	21,000
Retained Earnings b/f	0
Retained Earnings	0
Total Equity	**21,000**

Statement of Cash Flows	Period 1
Date From	01-Jan-27
Date To	31-Jan-27
Operating Cash	
Receipts from Customers	0
Payments to Staff	0
Payments to Suppliers	0
Loan Interest Payment	0
Income Taxes Paid	0
Net Operating Cash	**0**
Investing	
Payments for Fixed Assets	0
Financing	
Cash from Shareholders	21,000
Dividend Paid	0
Bank Loans Received	0
Loan Principle Repayments	0
Net Financing Cash Flow	**21,000**
Net Cash for The Period	**21,000**
Opening Cash	0
Closing Cash	**21,000**

Statement of Cash Flows

Financing Activities: Owner's Equity Contribution: This is reflected as an inflow under financing activities.

Income Statement

There is no impact on the income statement since the transaction does not involve revenue or expenses.

Balance Sheet

Assets: Current Assets: Cash increases.
Equity: Share Capital: The owner's equity contribution is reflected as an increase in Share Capital.
The increase in assets (cash) and equity (share capital) keeps the accounting equation balanced: Assets = Liabilities + Equity.

Event 02.01: The Business Receives a Loan From the Bank.

Event 02.01: The Business Receives a Loan From the Bank..

Commercial Purpose

The commercial purpose of receiving a $10,000 bank loan is to provide the business with additional funds for various operational needs, such as purchasing inventory, expanding operations, or covering other business expenses. This external financing boosts the company's cash reserves while creating a liability that must be repaid over time.

Source Documents

Loan Agreement: A formal agreement between the business and the bank detailing the loan amount, interest rate, repayment terms, and conditions.
Bank Deposit Slip: Evidence of the $10,000 cash deposit into the business bank account.

The business receives a loan from the bank.

Amount	10,000.00
Date	1/01/2027

Tees and Giggles Ltd

Financial Statements

Income Statement	Period 1
Date From	01-Jan-27
Date To	31-Jan-27
Sales Revenue	0
Cost of Sales	0
Gross Profit	**0**
Gross Profit Margin %	**0%**
Expenses	
Wages Expense	0
Wages Oncosts Expense	0
Electricity Expense	0
Rent Expense	0
Advertising Expense	0
Subscription Expense	0
Depreciation Expense	0
Total Expenses	**0**
Earning Before Interest and Taxation (EBIT)	**0**
EBIT Margin	**0%**
Interest Expense	0
Profit Before Tax (PBT)	**0**
Profit Before Tax Margin	**0%**
Income Tax Expense	**0**
Profit (-Loss) After Tax (PAT)	**0**
Profit (-Loss) After Tax %	**0%**

Checks	
Equity = Net Assets	TRUE
Cash Flow Cash = Balance Sheet Cash	TRUE
P&L Retained Earnings = P&L Retained Eranings	TRUE

Balance Sheet	Period 1
As At	31-Jan-27
Assets	
Current Assets	
Cash	10,000
Inventory/Stock	0
Accounts Receivable	0
Prepaid Expenses	0
Total Current Assets	**10,000**
Fixed Assets	
Fixed Assets	0
Accumulated Depreciation	0
Total Fixed Assets	**0**
Total Assets	**10,000**
Current Liabilities	
Accounts Payable	0
Deferred Revenue	0
Accrued Employee Costs	0
Provision for Income Tax	0
Total Current Liabilities	**0**
Long Term Liabilities	
Bank Loans	(10,000)
Total Liabilities	**(10,000)**
Net Assets	**0**
Equity	
Share Capital	0
Retained Earnings b/f	0
Retained Earnings	0
Total Equity	**0**

Statement of Cash Flows	Period 1
Date From	01-Jan-27
Date To	31-Jan-27
Operating Cash	
Receipts from Customers	0
Payments to Staff	0
Payments to Suppliers	0
Loan Interest Payment	0
Income Taxes Paid	0
Net Operating Cash	**0**
Investing	
Payments for Fixed Assets	0
Financing	
Cash from Shareholders	0
Dividend Paid	0
Bank Loans Received	10,000
Loan Principle Repayments	0
Net Financing Cash Flow	**10,000**
Net Cash for The Period	**10,000**
Opening Cash	0
Closing Cash	**10,000**

Statement of Cash Flows

Financing Activities: Bank Loan Received: This is reflected as an inflow of $10,000 under financing activities.
Net Cash for the Period: The total cash inflow for the period is $10,000.
Closing Cash: The ending cash balance for the period is $10,000, reflecting the loan received from the bank.

Income Statement

There is no impact on the income statement since the transaction does not involve revenue or expenses.

Balance Sheet

Assets: Current Assets: Cash increases by $10,000.
Liabilities: Long Term Liabilities: Bank Loans increase by $10,000.
The increase in assets (cash) and the corresponding increase in liabilities (bank loan) keep the accounting equation balanced: Assets = Liabilities + Equity.

Events 2.02, 2.03 and 2.04: First Instalment of Loan Repayment.

Events 2.02, 2.03 and 2.04: The Business Repays the first instalment of the Loan From the Bank.

Commercial Purpose

The commercial purpose of repaying the bank loan amounting to $439 is to fulfil the business's obligation to the lender, reducing the overall loan liability. This repayment includes an interest component of $42, which is the cost of borrowing, and a principal component of $397, which decreases the outstanding loan balance.

Source Documents

Bank Statement: Evidence of the $439 cash payment to the bank, showing both the interest and principal components.
Loan Agreement: Specifies the loan terms, including interest rate and repayment schedule.
Loan Agreement: A formal agreement between the business and the bank detailing the loan amount, interest rate, repayment terms, and conditions.
Bank Deposit Slip: Evidence of the $10,000 cash deposit into the business bank account.

Repay Bank Loan

Amount	439.00
Date	31/01/2027

Tees and Giggles Ltd

Financial Statements

Income Statement	Period 1
Date From	01-Jan-27
Date To	31-Jan-27
Sales Revenue	0
Cost of Sales	0
Gross Profit	**0**
Gross Profit Margin %	**0%**
Expenses	
Wages Expense	0
Wages Oncosts Expense	0
Electricity Expense	0
Rent Expense	0
Advertising Expense	0
Subscription Expense	0
Depreciation Expense	0
Total Expenses	**0**
Earning Before Interest and Taxation (EBIT)	**0**
EBIT Margin	**0%**
Interest Expense	(42)
Profit Before Tax (PBT)	**(42)**
Profit Before Tax Margin	**0%**
Income Tax Expense	**0**
Profit (-Loss) After Tax (PAT)	**(42)**
Profit (-Loss) After Tax %	**0%**

Checks	
Equity = Net Assets	TRUE
Cash Flow Cash = Balance Sheet Cash	TRUE
P&L Retained Earnings = P&L Retained Eranings	TRUE

Balance Sheet	Period 1
As At	31-Jan-27
Assets	
Current Assets	
Cash	(439)
Inventory/Stock	0
Accounts Receivable	0
Prepaid Expenses	0
Total Current Assets	**(439)**
Fixed Assets	
Fixed Assets	0
Accumulated Depreciation	0
Total Fixed Assets	**0**
Total Assets	**(439)**
Current Liabilities	
Accounts Payable	0
Deferred Revenue	0
Accrued Employee Costs	0
Provision for Income Tax	0
Total Current Liabilities	**0**
Long Term Liabilities	
Bank Loans	397
Total Liabilities	**397**
Net Assets	**(42)**
Equity	
Share Capital	0
Retained Earnings b/f	0
Retained Earnings	(42)
Total Equity	**(42)**

Statement of Cash Flows	Period 1
Date From	01-Jan-27
Date To	31-Jan-27
Operating Cash	
Receipts from Customers	0
Payments to Staff	0
Payments to Suppliers	0
Loan Interest Payment	(42)
Income Taxes Paid	0
Net Operating Cash	**(42)**
Investing	
Payments for Fixed Assets	0
Financing	
Cash from Shareholders	0
Dividend Paid	0
Bank Loans Received	0
Loan Principle Repayments	(397)
Net Financing Cash Flow	**(397)**
Net Cash for The Period	**(439)**
Opening Cash	**0**
Closing Cash	**(439)**

Statement of Cash Flows

Operating Activities:
Loan Interest Payment: Reflects an outflow of $42 for interest payment.
Net Operating Cash: Reflects an outflow of $42.
Financing Activities:
Loan Principal Repayment: Reflects an outflow of $397.
Net Cash for the Period: Reflects a total outflow of $439.
Closing Cash: The ending cash balance for the period is -$439, reflecting the payments made.

Income Statement

Interest Expense: The interest expense of $42 is recorded, increasing total expenses and resulting in a Loss Before Tax of $42.

Balance Sheet

Assets:
Current Assets: Cash decreases by $439.
Liabilities:
Long Term Liabilities: Bank Loans decrease by $397 due to the principal repayment portion of the payment.
Equity:
Retained Earnings: Decrease by $42, reflecting the net loss for the period.
The decrease in assets (cash) and the decrease in liabilities (bank loans) keep the accounting equation balanced: Assets = Liabilities + Equity.

Event 3.01: The Business Buys Inventory (Invoice Received).

Event 3.01: The Business Buys Inventory (Invoice Received).

Commercial Purpose

The commercial purpose of buying inventory (T-shirts) worth $5,000 is to stock up on goods for resale. This transaction increases the company's inventory levels, preparing the business for future Revenue generation.

Source Documents

Purchase Order: Document showing the order of inventory from the supplier.
Invoice: Supplier's bill for the inventory purchased.
Goods Received Note: Confirmation of the inventory received by the business.

The business buys inventory.

Amount	5,000.00
Date	15/01/2027

Tees and Giggles Ltd

Financial Statements

Income Statement	Period 1
Date From	01-Jan-27
Date To	31-Jan-27
Sales Revenue	0
Cost of Sales	0
Gross Profit	**0**
Gross Profit Margin %	**0%**
Expenses	
Wages Expense	0
Wages Oncosts Expense	0
Electricity Expense	0
Rent Expense	0
Advertising Expense	0
Subscription Expense	0
Depreciation Expense	0
Total Expenses	**0**
Earning Before Interest and Taxation (EBIT)	**0**
EBIT Margin	**0%**
Interest Expense	0
Profit Before Tax (PBT)	**0**
Profit Before Tax Margin	**0%**
Income Tax Expense	**0**
Profit (-Loss) After Tax (PAT)	**0**
Profit (-Loss) After Tax %	**0%**

Checks	
Equity = Net Assets	TRUE
Cash Flow Cash = Balance Sheet Cash	TRUE
P&L Retained Earnings = P&L Retained Eranings	TRUE

Balance Sheet	Period 1
As At	31-Jan-27
Assets	
Current Assets	
Cash	0
Inventory/Stock	5,000
Accounts Receivable	0
Prepaid Expenses	0
Total Current Assets	**5,000**
Fixed Assets	
Fixed Assets	0
Accumulated Depreciation	0
Total Fixed Assets	**0**
Total Assets	**5,000**
Current Liabilities	
Accounts Payable	(5,000)
Deferred Revenue	0
Accrued Employee Costs	0
Provision for Income Tax	0
Total Current Liabilities	**(5,000)**
Long Term Liabilities	
Bank Loans	0
Total Liabilities	**(5,000)**
Net Assets	**0**
Equity	
Share Capital	0
Retained Earnings b/f	0
Retained Earnings	0
Total Equity	**0**

Statement of Cash Flows	Period 1
Date From	01-Jan-27
Date To	31-Jan-27
Operating Cash	
Receipts from Customers	0
Payments to Staff	0
Payments to Suppliers	0
Loan Interest Payment	0
Income Taxes Paid	0
Net Operating Cash	**0**
Investing	
Payments for Fixed Assets	0
Financing	
Cash from Shareholders	0
Dividend Paid	0
Bank Loans Received	0
Loan Principle Repayments	0
Net Financing Cash Flow	**0**
Net Cash for The Period	**0**
Opening Cash	0
Closing Cash	0

Statement of Cash Flows

Statement of Cash Flows:
There is no impact on the statement of cash flows since the inventory purchase was made on credit and no cash was paid out during the period.

Income Statement

There is no impact on the income statement since the transaction does not involve revenue or expenses related to the period. All amounts remain at zero for the period.

Balance Sheet

Assets:
Current Assets: Inventory/Stock increases by $5,000.
Liabilities:
Current Liabilities: Accounts Payable increases by $5,000, reflecting the amount owed to the supplier.
The increase in assets (inventory) and the corresponding increase in liabilities (accounts payable) keep the accounting equation balanced: Assets = Liabilities + Equity.

Event 3.02: The Business Pays the Inventory Supplier.

Event 3.02: The Business Pays the Inventory Supplier.

Commercial Purpose

The commercial purpose of paying the inventory supplier $5,000 is to settle the outstanding accounts payable for the inventory previously purchased. This transaction reduces the business's liability and reflects the outflow of cash.

Source Documents

Payment Voucher: Document authorizing the payment to the supplier.
Bank Statement: Evidence of the $5,000 cash payment made to the supplier.

The business pays the Inventory supplier.

Amount	5,000.00
Date	25/01/2027

Tees and Giggles Ltd

Financial Statements

Income Statement	Period 1
Date From	01-Jan-27
Date To	31-Jan-27
Sales Revenue	0
Cost of Sales	0
Gross Profit	**0**
Gross Profit Margin %	**0%**
Expenses	
Wages Expense	0
Wages Oncosts Expense	0
Electricity Expense	0
Rent Expense	0
Advertising Expense	0
Subscription Expense	0
Depreciation Expense	0
Total Expenses	**0**
Earning Before Interest and Taxation (EBIT)	**0**
EBIT Margin	**0%**
Interest Expense	0
Profit Before Tax (PBT)	**0**
Profit Before Tax Margin	**0%**
Income Tax Expense	**0**
Profit (-Loss) After Tax (PAT)	**0**
Profit (-Loss) After Tax %	**0%**

Checks	
Equity = Net Assets	TRUE
Cash Flow Cash = Balance Sheet Cash	TRUE
P&L Retained Earnings = P&L Retained Eranings	TRUE

Balance Sheet	Period 1
As At	31-Jan-27
Assets	
Current Assets	
Cash	(5,000)
Inventory/Stock	0
Accounts Receivable	0
Prepaid Expenses	0
Total Current Assets	**(5,000)**
Fixed Assets	
Fixed Assets	0
Accumulated Depreciation	0
Total Fixed Assets	**0**
Total Assets	**(5,000)**
Current Liabilities	
Accounts Payable	5,000
Deferred Revenue	0
Accrued Employee Costs	0
Provision for Income Tax	0
Total Current Liabilities	**5,000**
Long Term Liabilities	
Bank Loans	0
Total Liabilities	**5,000**
Net Assets	**0**
Equity	
Share Capital	0
Retained Earnings b/f	0
Retained Earnings	0
Total Equity	**0**

Statement of Cash Flows	Period 1
Date From	01-Jan-27
Date To	31-Jan-27
Operating Cash	
Receipts from Customers	0
Payments to Staff	0
Payments to Suppliers	(5,000)
Loan Interest Payment	0
Income Taxes Paid	0
Net Operating Cash	**(5,000)**
Investing	
Payments for Fixed Assets	0
Financing	
Cash from Shareholders	0
Dividend Paid	0
Bank Loans Received	0
Loan Principle Repayments	0
Net Financing Cash Flow	**0**
Net Cash for The Period	**(5,000)**
Opening Cash	0
Closing Cash	**(5,000)**

Statement of Cash Flows

Operating Activities:
Payments to Suppliers: Reflects an outflow of $5,000 for the payment to the inventory supplier.
Net Operating Cash: Reflects an outflow of $5,000.
Net Cash for the Period: Reflects a total outflow of $5,000.
Closing Cash: The ending cash balance for the period is -$5,000, reflecting the payment made.

Income Statement

There is no impact on the income statement since the transaction does not involve revenue or expenses related to the period. All amounts remain at zero for the period.

Balance Sheet

Assets:
Current Assets: Cash decreases by $5,000.
Liabilities:
Current Liabilities: Accounts Payable decreases by $5,000, reflecting the payment made to the supplier.
The decrease in assets (cash) and the corresponding decrease in liabilities (accounts payable) keep the accounting equation balanced: Assets = Liabilities + Equity.

Event 4.01: The Business Invoices Customer for T-shirts sold.

Event 4.01: The Business Invoices Customer for T-shirts sold.

Commercial Purpose

The commercial purpose of earning revenue from sales amounting to $25,000 is to generate income for the business through its primary operations. This transaction increases the company's profitability and enhances its financial position by increasing both assets and equity.

Source Documents

Sales Invoice: Document issued to the customer detailing the sale and amount due.
Delivery Note: Confirmation of the goods delivered or services rendered to the customer.

The business earns revenue from sales.

Amount	25,000.00
Date	16/01/2027

Tees and Giggles Ltd

Financial Statements

Income Statement	Period 1
Date From	01-Jan-27
Date To	31-Jan-27
Sales Revenue	25,000
Cost of Sales	0
Gross Profit	**25,000**
Gross Profit Margin %	**100%**
Expenses	
Wages Expense	0
Wages Oncosts Expense	0
Electricity Expense	0
Rent Expense	0
Advertising Expense	0
Subscription Expense	0
Depreciation Expense	0
Total Expenses	**0**
Earning Before Interest and Taxation (EBIT)	**25,000**
EBIT Margin	**100%**
Interest Expense	0
Profit Before Tax (PBT)	**25,000**
Profit Before Tax Margin	**100%**
Income Tax Expense	**0**
Profit (-Loss) After Tax (PAT)	**25,000**
Profit (-Loss) After Tax %	**100%**

Checks	
Equity = Net Assets	TRUE
Cash Flow Cash = Balance Sheet Cash	TRUE
P&L Retained Earnings = P&L Retained Eranings	TRUE

Balance Sheet	Period 1
As At	31-Jan-27
Assets	
Current Assets	
Cash	0
Inventory/Stock	0
Accounts Receivable	25,000
Prepaid Expenses	0
Total Current Assets	**25,000**
Fixed Assets	
Fixed Assets	0
Accumulated Depreciation	0
Total Fixed Assets	**0**
Total Assets	**25,000**
Current Liabilities	
Accounts Payable	0
Deferred Revenue	0
Accrued Employee Costs	0
Provision for Income Tax	0
Total Current Liabilities	**0**
Long Term Liabilities	
Bank Loans	0
Total Liabilities	**0**
Net Assets	**25,000**
Equity	
Share Capital	0
Retained Earnings b/f	0
Retained Earnings	25,000
Total Equity	**25,000**

Statement of Cash Flows	Period 1
Date From	01-Jan-27
Date To	31-Jan-27
Operating Cash	
Receipts from Customers	0
Payments to Staff	0
Payments to Suppliers	0
Loan Interest Payment	0
Income Taxes Paid	0
Net Operating Cash	**0**
Investing	
Payments for Fixed Assets	0
Financing	
Cash from Shareholders	0
Dividend Paid	0
Bank Loans Received	0
Loan Principle Repayments	0
Net Financing Cash Flow	**0**
Net Cash for The Period	**0**
Opening Cash	0
Closing Cash	**0**

Statement of Cash Flows

There is no impact on the statement of cash flows since the sales were made on credit and no cash was received during the period.

Income Statement

Sales Revenue: The income statement records sales of $25,000.
Profit After Tax (PAT): Also reflects a profit of $25,000 as there are no other expenses or taxes recorded.

Balance Sheet

Assets:
Current Assets: Accounts Receivable increased by $25,000, reflecting the amount owed by customers.
Equity:
Retained Earnings: Increase by $25,000, reflecting the net profit from the sales.
The increase in assets (accounts receivable) and the corresponding increase in equity (retained earnings) keep the accounting equation balanced: Assets = Liabilities + Equity.

Event 4.02: Accounting Adjustment: Deferred Revenue. (200 units not delivered.)

Event 4.02: Accounting Adjustment: Deferred Revenue.

Commercial Purpose

The commercial purpose of deferring revenue is to comply with accounting principles, specifically the matching principle, which requires that revenue is recognised in the period it is earned, not necessarily when the cash is received. Deferring revenue ensures that financial statements reflect accurate and fair financial performance.

Source Documents

Sales Invoice: Document issued to the customer detailing the sale and amount due.
Delivery Note: Confirmation of the goods delivered or services rendered to the customer.

Business Event Details

Date of Transaction: 16-Jan-27
T-Shirts Sold: 1,000 units
Price Per Unit: $25
Units Delivered: 800 units
Total Invoice: $25,000
Recognized Sales: $20,000
Deferred Sales: $5,000 (200 units * $25)

for accounting purposes.

Date	31/01/2027

Tees and Giggles Ltd

Financial Statements

Income Statement	Period 1
Date From	01-Jan-27
Date To	31-Jan-27
Sales Revenue	(5,000)
Cost of Sales	0
Gross Profit	**(5,000)**
Gross Profit Margin %	**100%**
Expenses	
Wages Expense	0
Wages Oncosts Expense	0
Electricity Expense	0
Rent Expense	0
Advertising Expense	0
Subscription Expense	0
Depreciation Expense	0
Total Expenses	**0**
Earning Before Interest and Taxation (EBIT)	**(5,000)**
EBIT Margin	**100%**
Interest Expense	0
Profit Before Tax (PBT)	**(5,000)**
Profit Before Tax Margin	**100%**
Income Tax Expense	**0**
Profit (-Loss) After Tax (PAT)	**(5,000)**
Profit (-Loss) After Tax %	**100%**

Checks	
Equity = Net Assets	TRUE
Cash Flow Cash = Balance Sheet Cash	TRUE
P&L Retained Earnings = P&L Retained Eranings	TRUE

Balance Sheet	Period 1
As At	31-Jan-27
Assets	
Current Assets	
Cash	0
Inventory/Stock	0
Accounts Receivable	0
Prepaid Expenses	0
Total Current Assets	**0**
Fixed Assets	
Fixed Assets	0
Accumulated Depreciation	0
Total Fixed Assets	**0**
Total Assets	**0**
Current Liabilities	
Accounts Payable	0
Deferred Revenue	(5,000)
Accrued Employee Costs	0
Provision for Income Tax	0
Total Current Liabilities	**(5,000)**
Long Term Liabilities	
Bank Loans	0
Total Liabilities	**(5,000)**
Net Assets	**(5,000)**
Equity	
Share Capital	0
Retained Earnings b/f	0
Retained Earnings	(5,000)
Total Equity	**(5,000)**

Statement of Cash Flows	Period 1
Date From	01-Jan-27
Date To	31-Jan-27
Operating Cash	
Receipts from Customers	0
Payments to Staff	0
Payments to Suppliers	0
Loan Interest Payment	0
Income Taxes Paid	0
Net Operating Cash	**0**
Investing	
Payments for Fixed Assets	0
Financing	
Cash from Shareholders	0
Dividend Paid	0
Bank Loans Received	0
Loan Principle Repayments	0
Net Financing Cash Flow	**0**
Net Cash for The Period	**0**
Opening Cash	0
Closing Cash	**0**

Statement of Cash Flows

There is no impact on the statement of cash flows since the sales were made on credit and no cash was received during the period.

Income Statement

Sales Revenue: Deferred sales of $5,000 are subtracted, resulting in a negative impact on sales.

Balance Sheet

Assets:
Current Assets: No impact on cash or accounts receivable since the adjustment is for accounting purposes.
Liabilities:
Current Liabilities: Deferred Revenue increases by $5,000, reflecting the liability for revenue not yet recognized.
Equity:
Retained Earnings: Decrease by $5,000, reflecting the loss from the deferred revenue adjustment.
The increase in liabilities (deferred revenue) and the corresponding decrease in equity (retained earnings) keep the accounting equation balanced: Assets = Liabilities + Equity.

Event 4.03: The Business Receives Payments from Customers.

Event 4.03: The Business Receives Payments from Customers.

Commercial Purpose

The commercial purpose of receiving payments from customers amounting to $25,000 is to collect cash for the sales previously made on credit. This transaction increases the business's cash balance and reduces accounts receivable, improving liquidity.

Source Documents

Sales Invoice: Document issued to the customer detailing the sale.
Bank Statement: Evidence of the $25,000 cash received from customers.
Receipt: Issued to customers as proof of payment.

The business receives payments from customers.

Amount	25,000.00
Date	26/01/2027

Tees and Giggles Ltd

Financial Statements

Income Statement	Period 1
Date From	01-Jan-27
Date To	31-Jan-27
Sales Revenue	0
Cost of Sales	0
Gross Profit	**0**
Gross Profit Margin %	**0%**
Expenses	
Wages Expense	0
Wages Oncosts Expense	0
Electricity Expense	0
Rent Expense	0
Advertising Expense	0
Subscription Expense	0
Depreciation Expense	0
Total Expenses	**0**
Earning Before Interest and Taxation (EBIT)	**0**
EBIT Margin	**0%**
Interest Expense	0
Profit Before Tax (PBT)	**0**
Profit Before Tax Margin	**0%**
Income Tax Expense	**0**
Profit (-Loss) After Tax (PAT)	**0**
Profit (-Loss) After Tax %	**0%**

Checks	
Equity = Net Assets	TRUE
Cash Flow Cash = Balance Sheet Cash	TRUE
P&L Retained Earnings = P&L Retained Earnings	TRUE

Balance Sheet	Period 1
As At	31-Jan-27
Assets	
Current Assets	
Cash	25,000
Inventory/Stock	0
Accounts Receivable	(25,000)
Prepaid Expenses	0
Total Current Assets	**0**
Fixed Assets	
Fixed Assets	0
Accumulated Depreciation	0
Total Fixed Assets	**0**
Total Assets	**0**
Current Liabilities	
Accounts Payable	0
Deferred Revenue	0
Accrued Employee Costs	0
Provision for Income Tax	0
Total Current Liabilities	**0**
Long Term Liabilities	
Bank Loans	0
Total Liabilities	**0**
Net Assets	**0**
Equity	
Share Capital	0
Retained Earnings b/f	0
Retained Earnings	0
Total Equity	**0**

Statement of Cash Flows	Period 1
Date From	01-Jan-27
Date To	31-Jan-27
Operating Cash	
Receipts from Customers	25,000
Payments to Staff	0
Payments to Suppliers	0
Loan Interest Payment	0
Income Taxes Paid	0
Net Operating Cash	**25,000**
Investing	
Payments for Fixed Assets	0
Financing	
Cash from Shareholders	0
Dividend Paid	0
Bank Loans Received	0
Loan Principle Repayments	0
Net Financing Cash Flow	**0**
Net Cash for The Period	**25,000**
Opening Cash	**0**
Closing Cash	**25,000**

Statement of Cash Flows

Operating Activities:
Receipts from Customers: Reflects an inflow of $25,000 from the cash received.
Net Operating Cash: Reflects an inflow of $25,000.
Net Cash for the Period: Reflects a total inflow of $25,000.
Closing Cash: The ending cash balance for the period is $25,000, reflecting the payments received from customers.

Income Statement

There is no direct impact on the income statement from this transaction since the revenue was already recognised at the time of sale. This transaction only involves the collection of cash, not the recognition of new revenue or expenses.

Balance Sheet

Assets:
Current Assets: Cash increases by $25,000.
Accounts Receivable: Decreases by $25,000, reflecting the collection of cash from customers.
The increase in one current asset (cash) and the corresponding decrease in another current asset (accounts receivable) keep the accounting equation balanced: Assets = Liabilities + Equity.

Event 4.04: Accounting Adjustment – Cost of Goods Sold is Recognised

Event 4.04: Accounting Adjustment - Cost of Goods Sold is Recognised

Commercial Purpose

The commercial purpose of recognising the cost of goods sold is to match the cost of inventory with the revenue generated from selling that inventory. This ensures accurate reporting of gross profit and compliance with the matching principle in accounting.

Source Documents

Inventory Records: Document showing the cost of inventory sold.
Sales Invoice: Document detailing the sale of goods.
Delivery Note: Confirms the delivery of goods to the customer.

Business Event Details

Date of Transaction: 16-Jan-27
Price Per Unit: $25
Units Delivered: 800 units
Recognized Sales: $20,000 (800 x $25)
Cost of Sales: $4,000 (800x $5)

The cost of goods sold is recognised.

Amount	4,000.00
Date	31/01/2027

Tees and Giggles Ltd

Financial Statements

Income Statement	Period 1
Date From	01-Jan-27
Date To	31-Jan-27
Sales Revenue	0
Cost of Sales	(4,000)
Gross Profit	**(4,000)**
Gross Profit Margin %	**0%**
Expenses	
Wages Expense	0
Wages Oncosts Expense	0
Electricity Expense	0
Rent Expense	0
Advertising Expense	0
Subscription Expense	0
Depreciation Expense	0
Total Expenses	**0**
Earning Before Interest and Taxation (EBIT)	**(4,000)**
EBIT Margin	**0%**
Interest Expense	0
Profit Before Tax (PBT)	**(4,000)**
Profit Before Tax Margin	**0%**
Income Tax Expense	**0**
Profit (-Loss) After Tax (PAT)	**(4,000)**
Profit (-Loss) After Tax %	**0%**

Checks	
Equity = Net Assets	TRUE
Cash Flow Cash = Balance Sheet Cash	TRUE
P&L Retained Earnings = P&L Retained Eranings	TRUE

Balance Sheet	Period 1
As At	31-Jan-27
Assets	
Current Assets	
Cash	0
Inventory/Stock	(4,000)
Accounts Receivable	0
Prepaid Expenses	0
Total Current Assets	**(4,000)**
Fixed Assets	
Fixed Assets	0
Accumulated Depreciation	0
Total Fixed Assets	**0**
Total Assets	**(4,000)**
Current Liabilities	
Accounts Payable	0
Deferred Revenue	0
Accrued Employee Costs	0
Provision for Income Tax	0
Total Current Liabilities	**0**
Long Term Liabilities	
Bank Loans	0
Total Liabilities	**0**
Net Assets	**(4,000)**
Equity	
Share Capital	0
Retained Earnings b/f	0
Retained Earnings	(4,000)
Total Equity	**(4,000)**

Statement of Cash Flows	Period 1
Date From	01-Jan-27
Date To	31-Jan-27
Operating Cash	
Receipts from Customers	0
Payments to Staff	0
Payments to Suppliers	0
Loan Interest Payment	0
Income Taxes Paid	0
Net Operating Cash	**0**
Investing	
Payments for Fixed Assets	0
Financing	
Cash from Shareholders	0
Dividend Paid	0
Bank Loans Received	0
Loan Principle Repayments	0
Net Financing Cash Flow	**0**
Net Cash for The Period	**0**
Opening Cash	0
Closing Cash	**0**

Statement of Cash Flows

There is no impact on the statement of cash flows since the recognition of cost of goods sold is an accounting adjustment and does not involve cash transactions.

Income Statement

Cost of Sales (COGS): The income statement records a cost of sales of $4,000 (800 x $5).
Profit Before Tax (PBT): Reflects a loss of $4,000 due to the cost of goods sold.

Balance Sheet

Assets:
Current Assets: Inventory decreases by $4,000, reflecting the cost of goods sold.
Equity:
Retained Earnings: Decrease by $4,000, reflecting the net loss from the cost of goods sold.
The decrease in assets (inventory) and the corresponding decrease in equity (retained earnings) keep the accounting equation balanced: Assets = Liabilities + Equity.

Event 5.01: Business Buys Fixed Assets (Invoice Received)

Event 5.01: Business Buys Fixed Assets (Invoice Received)

Commercial Purpose

The commercial purpose of buying fixed assets is to invest in long-term resources used in business operations over several years. These assets will help generate revenue and are subject to depreciation over their useful life.

Source Documents

Purchase Invoice: Document detailing the purchase of fixed assets.
Fixed Asset Register: Records the details of the fixed assets, including cost, useful life, and depreciation.
Payment Receipt: Evidence of the payment made for the fixed assets.

Business Event Details

Date of Transaction: 03-Jan-27
Asset Purchased: T-shirt printing machine
Cost of Asset: $5,000
Effective Life: 36 months
Credit Days: 10 days
Payment Date: 13-Jan-27
Payment Amount: $5,000
Depreciation: $139.00 per month

The business b

Amount	5,000.00
Date	16/01/2027

Tees and Giggles Ltd

Financial Statements

Income Statement	Period 1
Date From	01-Jan-27
Date To	31-Jan-27
Sales Revenue	0
Cost of Sales	0
Gross Profit	**0**
Gross Profit Margin %	**0%**
Expenses	
Wages Expense	0
Wages Oncosts Expense	0
Electricity Expense	0
Rent Expense	0
Advertising Expense	0
Subscription Expense	0
Depreciation Expense	0
Total Expenses	**0**
Earning Before Interest and Taxation (EBIT)	**0**
EBIT Margin	**0%**
Interest Expense	0
Profit Before Tax (PBT)	**0**
Profit Before Tax Margin	**0%**
Income Tax Expense	**0**
Profit (-Loss) After Tax (PAT)	**0**
Profit (-Loss) After Tax %	**0%**

Checks	
Equity = Net Assets	TRUE
Cash Flow Cash = Balance Sheet Cash	TRUE
P&L Retained Earnings = P&L Retained Earnings	TRUE

Balance Sheet	Period 1
As At	31-Jan-27
Assets	
Current Assets	
Cash	0
Inventory/Stock	0
Accounts Receivable	0
Prepaid Expenses	0
Total Current Assets	**0**
Fixed Assets	
Fixed Assets	5,000
Accumulated Depreciation	0
Total Fixed Assets	**5,000**
Total Assets	**5,000**
Current Liabilities	
Accounts Payable	(5,000)
Deferred Revenue	0
Accrued Employee Costs	0
Provision for Income Tax	0
Total Current Liabilities	**(5,000)**
Long Term Liabilities	
Bank Loans	0
Total Liabilities	**(5,000)**
Net Assets	**0**
Equity	
Share Capital	0
Retained Earnings b/f	0
Retained Earnings	0
Total Equity	**0**

Statement of Cash Flows	Period 1
Date From	01-Jan-27
Date To	31-Jan-27
Operating Cash	
Receipts from Customers	0
Payments to Staff	0
Payments to Suppliers	0
Loan Interest Payment	0
Income Taxes Paid	0
Net Operating Cash	**0**
Investing	
Payments for Fixed Assets	0
Financing	
Cash from Shareholders	0
Dividend Paid	0
Bank Loans Received	0
Loan Principle Repayments	0
Net Financing Cash Flow	**0**
Net Cash for The Period	**0**
Opening Cash	0
Closing Cash	**0**

Statement of Cash Flows

There is no impact on the Statement of Cash Flows as the machine was purchased on credit.

Income Statement

There is no immediate impact on the income statement from the purchase of fixed assets since the expense is capitalised. However, depreciation expense will be recognised over the useful life of the asset, affecting future income statements.

Balance Sheet

Assets:
Fixed Assets: Increases by $5,000, reflecting the addition of the new machine.
Liabilities:
Current Liabilities: Accounts Payable increases by $5,000, reflecting the amount owed to the supplier.
The increase in fixed assets and the corresponding increase in liabilities (accounts payable) keep the accounting equation balanced: Assets = Liabilities + Equity.

Event 5.02: The Business Pays Fixed Asset Supplier

Event 5.02: The Business Pays Fixed Asset Supplier

Commercial Purpose

The commercial purpose of paying the fixed asset supplier $5,000 is to settle the outstanding accounts payable for the fixed assets previously purchased. This transaction reduces the business's liability and reflects the outflow of cash.

Source Documents

Payment Voucher: Document authorising the payment to the supplier.
Bank Statement: Evidence of the $5,000 cash payment made to the supplier.
Invoice: Supplier's bill for the fixed assets purchased.

The business pays the Fixed Asset supplier.

Amount	5,000.00
Date	26/01/2027

Tees and Giggles Ltd

Financial Statements

Income Statement	Period 1
Date From	01-Jan-27
Date To	31-Jan-27
Sales Revenue	0
Cost of Sales	0
Gross Profit	**0**
Gross Profit Margin %	**0%**
Expenses	
Wages Expense	0
Wages Oncosts Expense	0
Electricity Expense	0
Rent Expense	0
Advertising Expense	0
Subscription Expense	0
Depreciation Expense	0
Total Expenses	**0**
Earning Before Interest and Taxation (EBIT)	**0**
EBIT Margin	**0%**
Interest Expense	0
Profit Before Tax (PBT)	**0**
Profit Before Tax Margin	**0%**
Income Tax Expense	**0**
Profit (-Loss) After Tax (PAT)	**0**
Profit (-Loss) After Tax %	**0%**

Checks	
Equity = Net Assets	TRUE
Cash Flow Cash = Balance Sheet Cash	TRUE
P&L Retained Earnings = P&L Retained Eranings	TRUE

Balance Sheet	Period 1
As At	31-Jan-27
Assets	
Current Assets	
Cash	(5,000)
Inventory/Stock	0
Accounts Receivable	0
Prepaid Expenses	0
Total Current Assets	**(5,000)**
Fixed Assets	
Fixed Assets	0
Accumulated Depreciation	0
Total Fixed Assets	**0**
Total Assets	**(5,000)**
Current Liabilities	
Accounts Payable	5,000
Deferred Revenue	0
Accrued Employee Costs	0
Provision for Income Tax	0
Total Current Liabilities	**5,000**
Long Term Liabilities	
Bank Loans	0
Total Liabilities	**5,000**
Net Assets	**0**
Equity	
Share Capital	0
Retained Earnings b/f	0
Retained Earnings	0
Total Equity	**0**

Statement of Cash Flows	Period 1
Date From	01-Jan-27
Date To	31-Jan-27
Operating Cash	
Receipts from Customers	0
Payments to Staff	0
Payments to Suppliers	0
Loan Interest Payment	0
Income Taxes Paid	0
Net Operating Cash	**0**
Investing	
Payments for Fixed Assets	(5,000)
Financing	
Cash from Shareholders	0
Dividend Paid	0
Bank Loans Received	0
Loan Principle Repayments	0
Net Financing Cash Flow	**0**
Net Cash for The Period	**(5,000)**
Opening Cash	0
Closing Cash	**(5,000)**

Statement of Cash Flows

Investing Activities:
Payments for Fixed Assets: Reflects an outflow of $5,000 for the payment to the fixed asset supplier.
Net Cash for the Period: Reflects a total outflow of $5,000.
Closing Cash: The ending cash balance for the period is -$5,000, reflecting the payment made.

Income Statement

There is no direct impact on the income statement from this transaction since it involves the payment of a previously recorded liability and does not involve new revenue or expenses for the period.

Balance Sheet

Assets:
Current Assets: Cash decreases by $5,000.
Liabilities:
Current Liabilities: Accounts Payable decreased by $5,000, reflecting the payment made to the supplier.
The decrease in assets (cash) and the corresponding decrease in liabilities (accounts payable) keep the accounting equation balanced: Assets = Liabilities + Equity.

Event 5.03: Accounting Adjustment – Provision for Depreciation

Event 5.03: Accounting Adjustment - Provision for Depreciation

Commercial Purpose

The commercial purpose of recording depreciation on fixed assets is to allocate the cost of the asset over its useful life. Depreciation expense reflects the wear and tear, usage, or obsolescence of the fixed asset, ensuring that the expense is matched with the revenue generated by the asset.

Source Documents

Fixed Asset Register: Records the details of the fixed assets, including cost, useful life, and depreciation method.
Depreciation Schedule: Document detailing the calculation of depreciation for each asset.

Business Event Details

Date of Transaction: 31-Jan-27
Asset Purchased: T-shirt printing machine
Cost of Asset: $5,000
Effective Life: 36 months
Monthly Depreciation: $139.00

Depreciation is recorded on fixed assets.

Amount	139.00
Date	31/01/2027

Tees and Giggles Ltd

Financial Statements

Income Statement	Period 1
Date From	01-Jan-27
Date To	31-Jan-27
Sales Revenue	0
Cost of Sales	0
Gross Profit	**0**
Gross Profit Margin %	**0%**
Expenses	
Wages Expense	0
Wages Oncosts Expense	0
Electricity Expense	0
Rent Expense	0
Advertising Expense	0
Subscription Expense	0
Depreciation Expense	(139)
Total Expenses	**(139)**
Earning Before Interest and Taxation (EBIT)	**(139)**
EBIT Margin	**0%**
Interest Expense	0
Profit Before Tax (PBT)	**(139)**
Profit Before Tax Margin	**0%**
Income Tax Expense	**0**
Profit (-Loss) After Tax (PAT)	**(139)**
Profit (-Loss) After Tax %	**0%**

Balance Sheet	Period 1
As At	31-Jan-27
Assets	
Current Assets	
Cash	0
Inventory/Stock	0
Accounts Receivable	0
Prepaid Expenses	0
Total Current Assets	**0**
Fixed Assets	
Fixed Assets	0
Accumulated Depreciation	(139)
Total Fixed Assets	**(139)**
Total Assets	**(139)**
Current Liabilities	
Accounts Payable	0
Deferred Revenue	0
Accrued Employee Costs	0
Provision for Income Tax	0
Total Current Liabilities	**0**
Long Term Liabilities	
Bank Loans	0
Total Liabilities	**0**
Net Assets	**(139)**
Equity	
Share Capital	0
Retained Earnings b/f	0
Retained Earnings	(139)
Total Equity	**(139)**

Statement of Cash Flows	Period 1
Date From	01-Jan-27
Date To	31-Jan-27
Operating Cash	
Receipts from Customers	0
Payments to Staff	0
Payments to Suppliers	0
Loan Interest Payment	0
Income Taxes Paid	0
Net Operating Cash	**0**
Investing	
Payments for Fixed Assets	0
Financing	
Cash from Shareholders	0
Dividend Paid	0
Bank Loans Received	0
Loan Principle Repayments	0
Net Financing Cash Flow	**0**
Net Cash for The Period	**0**
Opening Cash	**0**
Closing Cash	**0**

Checks	
Equity = Net Assets	TRUE
Cash Flow Cash = Balance Sheet Cash	TRUE
P&L Retained Earnings = P&L Retained Eranings	TRUE

Statement of Cash Flows

There is no impact on the statement of cash flows since depreciation is a non-cash expense. It is an accounting adjustment to reflect the allocation of the cost of the fixed asset over its useful life.

Income Statement

Depreciation Expense: The income statement records a depreciation expense of $139.
Total Expenses: Reflect the addition of depreciation expense.
Profit Before Tax (PBT): Reflects a loss of $139 due to the depreciation expense.

Balance Sheet

Assets:
Fixed Assets: The value of the fixed asset (shelves) remains the same, but Accumulated Depreciation increases by $139, reducing the net book value of the fixed asset.
Equity:
Retained Earnings: Decrease by $139, reflecting the net loss from the depreciation expense.
The increase in accumulated depreciation (a contra asset account) and the corresponding decrease in equity (retained earnings) keep the accounting equation balanced: Assets = Liabilities + Equity.

Event 6.01: The Business Buys Software Subscription (Invoice Received)

Event 6.01: The business buys software subscription (Invoice Received)

Commercial Purpose

The commercial purpose of prepaying for software subscription expenses is to secure access to essential software services for the business over the next 12 months.

Source Documents

Supplier invoice showing the value of the purchase and confirmation of the duration of service, in this case 12 months.

Business Event Details

Date of Transaction: 3-Jan-27
Computer Software Subscription Purchase
Cost of Asset: $24,000
Service Period: 12 months
Monthly Depreciation: $2,000

The business prepays for Software Subscription Expenses for 12 Months.

Amount	24,000.00
Date	3/01/2027

Tees and Giggles Ltd

Financial Statements

Income Statement	Period 1
Date From	01-Jan-27
Date To	31-Jan-27
Sales Revenue	0
Cost of Sales	0
Gross Profit	**0**
Gross Profit Margin %	**0%**
Expenses	
Wages Expense	0
Wages Oncosts Expense	0
Electricity Expense	0
Rent Expense	0
Advertising Expense	0
Subscription Expense	0
Depreciation Expense	0
Total Expenses	**0**
Earning Before Interest and Taxation (EBIT)	**0**
EBIT Margin	**0%**
Interest Expense	0
Profit Before Tax (PBT)	**0**
Profit Before Tax Margin	**0%**
Income Tax Expense	**0**
Profit (-Loss) After Tax (PAT)	**0**
Profit (-Loss) After Tax %	**0%**

Checks	
Equity = Net Assets	TRUE
Cash Flow Cash = Balance Sheet Cash	TRUE
P&L Retained Earnings = P&L Retained Eranings	TRUE

Balance Sheet	Period 1
As At	31-Jan-27
Assets	
Current Assets	
Cash	0
Inventory/Stock	0
Accounts Receivable	0
Prepaid Expenses	24,000
Total Current Assets	**24,000**
Fixed Assets	
Fixed Assets	0
Accumulated Depreciation	0
Total Fixed Assets	**0**
Total Assets	**24,000**
Current Liabilities	
Accounts Payable	(24,000)
Deferred Revenue	0
Accrued Employee Costs	0
Provision for Income Tax	0
Total Current Liabilities	**(24,000)**
Long Term Liabilities	
Bank Loans	0
Total Liabilities	**(24,000)**
Net Assets	**0**
Equity	
Share Capital	0
Retained Earnings b/f	0
Retained Earnings	0
Total Equity	**0**

Statement of Cash Flows	Period 1
Date From	01-Jan-27
Date To	31-Jan-27
Operating Cash	
Receipts from Customers	0
Payments to Staff	0
Payments to Suppliers	0
Loan Interest Payment	0
Income Taxes Paid	0
Net Operating Cash	**0**
Investing	
Payments for Fixed Assets	0
Financing	
Cash from Shareholders	0
Dividend Paid	0
Bank Loans Received	0
Loan Principle Repayments	0
Net Financing Cash Flow	**0**
Net Cash for The Period	**0**
Opening Cash	0
Closing Cash	**0**

Statement of Cash Flows

There is no impact on the statement of cash flows since depreciation is a non-cash expense. It is an accounting adjustment to reflect the allocation of the cost of the fixed asset over its useful life.

Income Statement

There is no Impact to the Income Statement.

Balance Sheet

Assets:
Prepaid Expenses: Prepaid Expenses is increased recognising as expense and is used for more than a month.
Liabilities:
Accounts payable increases recognising the payment due to the software supplier.

Event 6.02: The Business Pays Software Subscription Supplier

Event 6.02: The Business Pays Software Subscription Supplier

Commercial Purpose

The commercial purpose of paying the computer software supplier $24,000 is to settle the outstanding accounts payable for the prepaid software subscription expenses. This payment ensures that the business has fulfilled its obligation to the supplier, securing the software services for the next 12 months.

Source Documents

Payment Voucher: Document authorising the payment to the software supplier.
Bank Statement: Evidence of the $24,000 cash payment made to the supplier.
Invoice: Supplier's bill for the software subscription services.

The business pays the Computer Software Supplier.

Amount	24,000.00
Date	13/01/2027

Tees and Giggles Ltd

Financial Statements

Income Statement	Period 1
Date From	01-Jan-27
Date To	31-Jan-27
Sales Revenue	0
Cost of Sales	0
Gross Profit	**0**
Gross Profit Margin %	**0%**
Expenses	
Wages Expense	0
Wages Oncosts Expense	0
Electricity Expense	0
Rent Expense	0
Advertising Expense	0
Subscription Expense	0
Depreciation Expense	0
Total Expenses	**0**
Earning Before Interest and Taxation (EBIT)	**0**
EBIT Margin	**0%**
Interest Expense	0
Profit Before Tax (PBT)	**0**
Profit Before Tax Margin	**0%**
Income Tax Expense	**0**
Profit (-Loss) After Tax (PAT)	**0**
Profit (-Loss) After Tax %	**0%**

Checks	
Equity = Net Assets	TRUE
Cash Flow Cash = Balance Sheet Cash	TRUE
P&L Retained Earnings = P&L Retained Eranings	TRUE

Balance Sheet	Period 1
As At	31-Jan-27
Assets	
Current Assets	
Cash	(24,000)
Inventory/Stock	0
Accounts Receivable	0
Prepaid Expenses	0
Total Current Assets	**(24,000)**
Fixed Assets	
Fixed Assets	0
Accumulated Depreciation	0
Total Fixed Assets	**0**
Total Assets	**(24,000)**
Current Liabilities	
Accounts Payable	24,000
Deferred Revenue	0
Accrued Employee Costs	0
Provision for Income Tax	0
Total Current Liabilities	**24,000**
Long Term Liabilities	
Bank Loans	0
Total Liabilities	**24,000**
Net Assets	**0**
Equity	
Share Capital	0
Retained Earnings b/f	0
Retained Earnings	0
Total Equity	**0**

Statement of Cash Flows	Period 1
Date From	01-Jan-27
Date To	31-Jan-27
Operating Cash	
Receipts from Customers	0
Payments to Staff	0
Payments to Suppliers	(24,000)
Loan Interest Payment	0
Income Taxes Paid	0
Net Operating Cash	**(24,000)**
Investing	
Payments for Fixed Assets	0
Financing	
Cash from Shareholders	0
Dividend Paid	0
Bank Loans Received	0
Loan Principle Repayments	0
Net Financing Cash Flow	**0**
Net Cash for The Period	**(24,000)**
Opening Cash	**0**
Closing Cash	**(24,000)**

Statement of Cash Flows

Operating Activities:
Payments to Suppliers: Reflects an outflow of $24,000 for the payment to the software supplier.
Net Operating Cash: Reflects an outflow of $24,000.
Net Cash for the Period: Reflects a total outflow of $24,000.
Closing Cash: The ending cash balance for the period is -$24,000, reflecting the payment made.

Income Statement

There is no direct impact on the income statement from this transaction since it involves the payment of a previously recorded liability (prepaid expense) and does not involve new revenue or expenses for the period.

Balance Sheet

Assets:
Current Assets: Cash decreases by $24,000, reflecting the payment made.
Prepaid Expenses: Remains the same at $24,000, as it still reflects the prepaid software subscription for the next 12 months.
Liabilities:
Current Liabilities: Accounts Payable decreases by $24,000, reflecting the settlement of the liability.
The decrease in one current asset (cash) and the corresponding decrease in current liabilities (accounts payable) keep the accounting equation balanced: Assets = Liabilities + Equity.

Event 6.03: Accounting Adjustment – Expense Prepaid Subscription

Event 6.03: Accounting Adjustment - Expense Prepaid Subscription

Commercial Purpose

The commercial purpose of recognising the prepaid subscription expense is to allocate the cost of the software subscription over its usage period. This ensures that the expense is matched with the period in which the benefit is received, in line with the matching principle in accounting. In this case monthly expense ($24,000 divided by 12 months) = $2,000.

Source Documents

Subscription Agreement: Document detailing the terms and period of the software subscription.
Prepaid Expense Schedule: Record of the prepaid subscription and the portion to be expensed each period.

The prepaid subscription expense is recognised.

Amount	2,000.00
Date	31/01/2027

Tees and Giggles Ltd

Financial Statements

Income Statement	Period 1
Date From	01-Jan-27
Date To	31-Jan-27
Sales Revenue	0
Cost of Sales	0
Gross Profit	**0**
Gross Profit Margin %	**0%**
Expenses	
Wages Expense	0
Wages Oncosts Expense	0
Electricity Expense	0
Rent Expense	0
Advertising Expense	0
Subscription Expense	(2,000)
Depreciation Expense	0
Total Expenses	**(2,000)**
Earning Before Interest and Taxation (EBIT)	**(2,000)**
EBIT Margin	**0%**
Interest Expense	0
Profit Before Tax (PBT)	**(2,000)**
Profit Before Tax Margin	**0%**
Income Tax Expense	**0**
Profit (-Loss) After Tax (PAT)	**(2,000)**
Profit (-Loss) After Tax %	**0%**

Checks	
Equity = Net Assets	TRUE
Cash Flow Cash = Balance Sheet Cash	TRUE
P&L Retained Earnings = P&L Retained Eranings	TRUE

Balance Sheet	Period 1
As At	31-Jan-27
Assets	
Current Assets	
Cash	0
Inventory/Stock	0
Accounts Receivable	0
Prepaid Expenses	(2,000)
Total Current Assets	**(2,000)**
Fixed Assets	
Fixed Assets	0
Accumulated Depreciation	0
Total Fixed Assets	**0**
Total Assets	**(2,000)**
Current Liabilities	
Accounts Payable	0
Deferred Revenue	0
Accrued Employee Costs	0
Provision for Income Tax	0
Total Current Liabilities	**0**
Long Term Liabilities	
Bank Loans	0
Total Liabilities	**0**
Net Assets	**(2,000)**
Equity	
Share Capital	0
Retained Earnings b/f	0
Retained Earnings	(2,000)
Total Equity	**(2,000)**

Statement of Cash Flows	Period 1
Date From	01-Jan-27
Date To	31-Jan-27
Operating Cash	
Receipts from Customers	0
Payments to Staff	0
Payments to Suppliers	0
Loan Interest Payment	0
Income Taxes Paid	0
Net Operating Cash	**0**
Investing	
Payments for Fixed Assets	0
Financing	
Cash from Shareholders	0
Dividend Paid	0
Bank Loans Received	0
Loan Principle Repayments	0
Net Financing Cash Flow	**0**
Net Cash for The Period	**0**
Opening Cash	**0**
Closing Cash	**0**

Statement of Cash Flows

There is no impact on the statement of cash flows since the recognition of prepaid subscription expense is an accounting adjustment and does not involve cash transactions.

Income Statement

Subscription Expense: The income statement records a subscription expense of $2,000 for the month.
Total Expenses: Reflect the addition of the subscription expense.
Profit Before Tax (PBT): Reflects a loss of $2,000 due to the subscription expense.

Balance Sheet

Assets:
Current Assets: Prepaid Expenses decrease by $2,000, reflecting the portion of the subscription used during the period.
Equity:
Retained Earnings: Decrease by $2,000, reflecting the net loss from the subscription expense.
The decrease in prepaid expenses (an asset) and the corresponding decrease in equity (retained earnings) keep the accounting equation balanced: Assets = Liabilities + Equity.

Event 7.01: The Business Incurs Salaries and Wages Expenses.

Event 7.01: The Business Incurs Salaries and Wages Expenses.

Commercial Purpose

The commercial purpose of incurring salaries and wages expense is to compensate employees for their work during the period. This expense is necessary for the business to maintain operations and support revenue generation.

Source Documents

Payroll Register: Document detailing the salaries and wages paid to employees.
Bank Statement: Evidence of the $5,000 cash payment made for salaries and wages.
Payment Vouchers: Documents authorising the payment of salaries and wages.

The business incurs salaries and wages expense.

Amount	5,000.00
Date	3/01/2027

Tees and Giggles Ltd

Financial Statements

Income Statement	Period 1
Date From	01-Jan-27
Date To	31-Jan-27
Sales Revenue	0
Cost of Sales	0
Gross Profit	**0**
Gross Profit Margin %	**0%**
Expenses	
Wages Expense	(5,000)
Wages Oncosts Expense	0
Electricity Expense	0
Rent Expense	0
Advertising Expense	0
Subscription Expense	0
Depreciation Expense	0
Total Expenses	**(5,000)**
Earning Before Interest and Taxation (EBIT)	**(5,000)**
EBIT Margin	**0%**
Interest Expense	0
Profit Before Tax (PBT)	**(5,000)**
Profit Before Tax Margin	**0%**
Income Tax Expense	**0**
Profit (-Loss) After Tax (PAT)	**(5,000)**
Profit (-Loss) After Tax %	**0%**

Balance Sheet	Period 1
As At	31-Jan-27
Assets	
Current Assets	
Cash	(5,000)
Inventory/Stock	0
Accounts Receivable	0
Prepaid Expenses	0
Total Current Assets	**(5,000)**
Fixed Assets	
Fixed Assets	0
Accumulated Depreciation	0
Total Fixed Assets	**0**
Total Assets	**(5,000)**
Current Liabilities	
Accounts Payable	0
Deferred Revenue	0
Accrued Employee Costs	0
Provision for Income Tax	0
Total Current Liabilities	**0**
Long Term Liabilities	
Bank Loans	0
Total Liabilities	**0**
Net Assets	**(5,000)**
Equity	
Share Capital	0
Retained Earnings b/f	0
Retained Earnings	(5,000)
Total Equity	**(5,000)**

Statement of Cash Flows	Period 1
Date From	01-Jan-27
Date To	31-Jan-27
Operating Cash	
Receipts from Customers	0
Payments to Staff	(5,000)
Payments to Suppliers	0
Loan Interest Payment	0
Income Taxes Paid	0
Net Operating Cash	**(5,000)**
Investing	
Payments for Fixed Assets	0
Financing	
Cash from Shareholders	0
Dividend Paid	0
Bank Loans Received	0
Loan Principle Repayments	0
Net Financing Cash Flow	**0**
Net Cash for The Period	**(5,000)**
Opening Cash	0
Closing Cash	**(5,000)**

Checks	
Equity = Net Assets	TRUE
Cash Flow Cash = Balance Sheet Cash	TRUE
P&L Retained Earnings = P&L Retained Eranings	TRUE

Statement of Cash Flows

Operating Activities:
Payments to Staff: Reflects an outflow of $5,000 for the payment of salaries and wages.
Net Operating Cash: Reflects an outflow of $5,000.
Net Cash for the Period: Reflects a total outflow of $5,000.
Closing Cash: The ending cash balance for the period is -$5,000, reflecting the payment made.

Income Statement

Wages Expense: The income statement records a wages expense of $5,000.
Total Expenses: Reflect the addition of the wages expense.
Profit Before Tax (PBT): Reflects a loss of $5,000 due to the wages expense.

Balance Sheet

Assets:
Current Assets: Cash decreases by $5,000, reflecting the payment made.
Equity:
Retained Earnings: Decrease by $5,000, reflecting the net loss from the wages expense.
The decrease in assets (cash) and the corresponding decrease in equity (retained earnings) keep the accounting equation balanced: Assets = Liabilities + Equity.

Event 7.02: Accounting Adjustment – Accrued Payroll On-costs

Event 7.02: Accounting Adjustment - Accrued Payroll On-costs

Commercial Purpose

The commercial purpose of recognising accrued oncosts for salaries is to accurately match the cost of employment-related expenses with the period in which they are incurred. This ensures that the financial statements reflect the true cost of employing staff, including additional costs like payroll taxes and other benefits.

Source Documents

Payroll Register: Document detailing the salaries, wages, and associated oncosts calculated based on contract of employment and employment and tax legislation.
Accrued Expenses Schedule: Record of accrued expenses and the portion to be recognised each period.
Payment Vouchers: Documents authorising the payment of oncosts when due.

Business Event Details

Date of Transaction: 03-Jan-27
Wages: $5,000
Oncosts Percentage: 20%
Oncosts Expense: $1,000 (20% of $5,000)
Payment Date for Wages: 03-Jan-27
Credit Days for Oncosts: 10 days
Payment Date for Oncosts: 13-Jan-27
Payment Amount for Oncosts: $1,000

Date 3/01/2027

Tees and Giggles Ltd

Financial Statements

Income Statement	Period 1
Date From	01-Jan-27
Date To	31-Jan-27
Sales Revenue	0
Cost of Sales	0
Gross Profit	**0**
Gross Profit Margin %	**0%**
Expenses	
Wages Expense	0
Wages Oncosts Expense	(1,000)
Electricity Expense	0
Rent Expense	0
Advertising Expense	0
Subscription Expense	0
Depreciation Expense	0
Total Expenses	**(1,000)**
Earning Before Interest and Taxation (EBIT)	**(1,000)**
EBIT Margin	**0%**
Interest Expense	0
Profit Before Tax (PBT)	**(1,000)**
Profit Before Tax Margin	**0%**
Income Tax Expense	**0**
Profit (-Loss) After Tax (PAT)	**(1,000)**
Profit (-Loss) After Tax %	**0%**

Checks	
Equity = Net Assets	TRUE
Cash Flow Cash = Balance Sheet Cash	TRUE
P&L Retained Earnings = P&L Retained Earnings	TRUE

Balance Sheet	Period 1
As At	31-Jan-27
Assets	
Current Assets	
Cash	0
Inventory/Stock	0
Accounts Receivable	0
Prepaid Expenses	0
Total Current Assets	**0**
Fixed Assets	
Fixed Assets	0
Accumulated Depreciation	0
Total Fixed Assets	**0**
Total Assets	**0**
Current Liabilities	
Accounts Payable	0
Deferred Revenue	0
Accrued Employee Costs	(1,000)
Provision for Income Tax	0
Total Current Liabilities	**(1,000)**
Long Term Liabilities	
Bank Loans	0
Total Liabilities	**(1,000)**
Net Assets	**(1,000)**
Equity	
Share Capital	0
Retained Earnings b/f	0
Retained Earnings	(1,000)
Total Equity	**(1,000)**

Statement of Cash Flows	Period 1
Date From	01-Jan-27
Date To	31-Jan-27
Operating Cash	
Receipts from Customers	0
Payments to Staff	0
Payments to Suppliers	0
Loan Interest Payment	0
Income Taxes Paid	0
Net Operating Cash	**0**
Investing	
Payments for Fixed Assets	0
Financing	
Cash from Shareholders	0
Dividend Paid	0
Bank Loans Received	0
Loan Principle Repayments	0
Net Financing Cash Flow	**0**
Net Cash for The Period	**0**
Opening Cash	0
Closing Cash	**0**

Statement of Cash Flows

There is no immediate impact on the statement of cash flows since the recognition of accrued oncosts is an accounting adjustment and does not involve cash transactions. The cash impact will be recorded when the payment is made on the due date.

Income Statement

Wages Oncosts Expense: The income statement records an oncosts expense of $1,000 for the period.
Total Expenses: Reflect the addition of the oncosts expense.
Profit Before Tax (PBT): Reflects a loss of $1,000 due to the oncosts expense.

Balance Sheet

Liabilities:
Current Liabilities: Accrued Employee Costs increase by $1,000, reflecting the obligation to pay oncosts.
Equity:
Retained Earnings: Decrease by $1,000, reflecting the net loss from the oncosts expense.
The increase in liabilities (accrued employee costs) and the corresponding decrease in equity (retained earnings) keep the accounting equation balanced: Assets = Liabilities + Equity.

Event 7.03 The Business Pays Accrued Payroll Oncosts

Event 7.03 The Business Pays Accrued Payroll Oncosts

Commercial Purpose

The commercial purpose of paying accrued on-costs for salaries is to settle the previously recorded liability related to employment-related expenses such as payroll taxes and other benefits. This payment ensures that the business fulfils its obligations to the relevant authorities or service providers.

Source Documents

Payment Voucher: Document authorising the payment of accrued on-costs.
Bank Statement: Evidence of the $1,000 cash payment made for the on-costs.
Payroll Register: Document detailing the salaries, wages, and associated on-costs.

The business pays Accrued oncosts for Salaries.

Amount	1,000.00
Date	13/01/2027

Tees and Giggles Ltd

Financial Statements

Income Statement	Period 1
Date From	01-Jan-27
Date To	31-Jan-27
Sales Revenue	0
Cost of Sales	0
Gross Profit	**0**
Gross Profit Margin %	**0%**
Expenses	
Wages Expense	0
Wages Oncosts Expense	0
Electricity Expense	0
Rent Expense	0
Advertising Expense	0
Subscription Expense	0
Depreciation Expense	0
Total Expenses	**0**
Earning Before Interest and Taxation (EBIT)	**0**
EBIT Margin	**0%**
Interest Expense	0
Profit Before Tax (PBT)	**0**
Profit Before Tax Margin	**0%**
Income Tax Expense	**0**
Profit (-Loss) After Tax (PAT)	**0**
Profit (-Loss) After Tax %	**0%**

Checks	
Equity = Net Assets	TRUE
Cash Flow Cash = Balance Sheet Cash	TRUE
P&L Retained Earnings = P&L Retained Eranings	TRUE

Balance Sheet	Period 1
As At	31-Jan-27
Assets	
Current Assets	
Cash	(1,000)
Inventory/Stock	0
Accounts Receivable	0
Prepaid Expenses	0
Total Current Assets	**(1,000)**
Fixed Assets	
Fixed Assets	0
Accumulated Depreciation	0
Total Fixed Assets	**0**
Total Assets	**(1,000)**
Current Liabilities	
Accounts Payable	0
Deferred Revenue	0
Accrued Employee Costs	1,000
Provision for Income Tax	0
Total Current Liabilities	**1,000**
Long Term Liabilities	
Bank Loans	0
Total Liabilities	**1,000**
Net Assets	**0**
Equity	
Share Capital	0
Retained Earnings b/f	0
Retained Earnings	0
Total Equity	**0**

Statement of Cash Flows	Period 1
Date From	01-Jan-27
Date To	31-Jan-27
Operating Cash	
Receipts from Customers	0
Payments to Staff	(1,000)
Payments to Suppliers	0
Loan Interest Payment	0
Income Taxes Paid	0
Net Operating Cash	**(1,000)**
Investing	
Payments for Fixed Assets	0
Financing	
Cash from Shareholders	0
Dividend Paid	0
Bank Loans Received	0
Loan Principle Repayments	0
Net Financing Cash Flow	**0**
Net Cash for The Period	**(1,000)**
Opening Cash	**0**
Closing Cash	**(1,000)**

Statement of Cash Flows

Operating Activities:
Payments to Staff: Reflects an outflow of $1,000 for the payment of the accrued on-costs.
Net Operating Cash: Reflects an outflow of $1,000.
Net Cash for the Period: Reflects a total outflow of $1,000.
Closing Cash: The ending cash balance for the period is -$1,000, reflecting the payment made.

Income Statement

There is no direct impact on the income statement from this transaction since it involves the payment of a previously recorded liability and does not involve new revenue or expenses for the period.

Balance Sheet

Assets:
Current Assets: Cash decreases by $1,000, reflecting the payment made.
Liabilities:
Current Liabilities: Accrued Employee Costs decrease by $1,000, reflecting the settlement of the liability.
The decrease in one current asset (cash) and the corresponding decrease in current liabilities (accrued employee costs) keep the accounting equation balanced: Assets = Liabilities + Equity.

Event 8.01: The Business Incurs Electricity Expense (Invoice Received)

Event 8.01: The Business Incurs Electricity Expense (Invoice Received)

Commercial Purpose

The commercial purpose of incurring electricity expense is to account for the cost of electricity used during the period. This expense is necessary for the business to maintain its operations, such as lighting, heating, and powering equipment.

Source Documents

Electricity Bill: Document detailing the cost of electricity consumed during the billing period.
Payment Voucher: Document authorising the payment of the electricity bill.
Bank Statement: Evidence of the $1,000 payment made for the electricity bill.

The business incurs electricity expense.

Amount	1,000.00
Date	3/01/2027

Tees and Giggles Ltd

Financial Statements

Income Statement	Period 1
Date From	01-Jan-27
Date To	31-Jan-27
Sales Revenue	0
Cost of Sales	0
Gross Profit	**0**
Gross Profit Margin %	**0%**
Expenses	
Wages Expense	0
Wages Oncosts Expense	0
Electricity Expense	(1,000)
Rent Expense	0
Advertising Expense	0
Subscription Expense	0
Depreciation Expense	0
Total Expenses	**(1,000)**
Earning Before Interest and Taxation (EBIT)	**(1,000)**
EBIT Margin	**0%**
Interest Expense	0
Profit Before Tax (PBT)	**(1,000)**
Profit Before Tax Margin	**0%**
Income Tax Expense	**0**
Profit (-Loss) After Tax (PAT)	**(1,000)**
Profit (-Loss) After Tax %	**0%**

Checks	
Equity = Net Assets	TRUE
Cash Flow Cash = Balance Sheet Cash	TRUE
P&L Retained Earnings = P&L Retained Earnings	TRUE

Balance Sheet	Period 1
As At	31-Jan-27
Assets	
Current Assets	
Cash	0
Inventory/Stock	0
Accounts Receivable	0
Prepaid Expenses	0
Total Current Assets	**0**
Fixed Assets	
Fixed Assets	0
Accumulated Depreciation	0
Total Fixed Assets	**0**
Total Assets	**0**
Current Liabilities	
Accounts Payable	(1,000)
Deferred Revenue	0
Accrued Employee Costs	0
Provision for Income Tax	0
Total Current Liabilities	**(1,000)**
Long Term Liabilities	
Bank Loans	0
Total Liabilities	**(1,000)**
Net Assets	**(1,000)**
Equity	
Share Capital	0
Retained Earnings b/f	0
Retained Earnings	(1,000)
Total Equity	**(1,000)**

Statement of Cash Flows	Period 1
Date From	01-Jan-27
Date To	31-Jan-27
Operating Cash	
Receipts from Customers	0
Payments to Staff	0
Payments to Suppliers	0
Loan Interest Payment	0
Income Taxes Paid	0
Net Operating Cash	**0**
Investing	
Payments for Fixed Assets	0
Financing	
Cash from Shareholders	0
Dividend Paid	0
Bank Loans Received	0
Loan Principle Repayments	0
Net Financing Cash Flow	**0**
Net Cash for The Period	**0**
Opening Cash	0
Closing Cash	**0**

Statement of Cash Flows

There is no immediate impact on the statement of cash flows since the expense has been incurred but not yet paid. The cash impact will be recorded when the payment is made.

Income Statement

Electricity Expense: The income statement records an electricity expense of $1,000 for the period.
Total Expenses: Reflect the addition of the electricity expense.
Profit Before Tax (PBT): Reflects a loss of $1,000 due to the electricity expense.

Balance Sheet

Liabilities:
Current Liabilities: Accounts Payable increase by $1,000, reflecting the obligation to pay the electricity supplier.
Equity:
Retained Earnings: Decrease by $1,000, reflecting the net loss from the electricity expense.
The increase in liabilities (accounts payable) and the corresponding decrease in equity (retained earnings) keep the accounting equation balanced: Assets = Liabilities + Equity.

Event 8.02: Business Pays Electricity Supplier

Event 8.02: Business Pays Electricity Supplier

Commercial Purpose

The commercial purpose of paying the electricity supplier $1,000 is to settle the outstanding accounts payable for the electricity expense previously incurred. This payment ensures that the business fulfils its obligation to the supplier and maintains a good credit relationship.

Source Documents

Payment Voucher: Document authorising the payment to the electricity supplier.
Bank Statement: Evidence of the $1,000 cash payment made to the supplier.
Electricity Bill: Document detailing the cost of electricity consumed and previously recorded as an expense.

The business pays the electricity supplier.

Amount	1,000.00
Date	13/01/2027

Tees and Giggles Ltd

Financial Statements

Income Statement	Period 1
Date From	01-Jan-27
Date To	31-Jan-27
Sales Revenue	0
Cost of Sales	0
Gross Profit	**0**
Gross Profit Margin %	**0%**
Expenses	
Wages Expense	0
Wages Oncosts Expense	0
Electricity Expense	0
Rent Expense	0
Advertising Expense	0
Subscription Expense	0
Depreciation Expense	0
Total Expenses	**0**
Earning Before Interest and Taxation (EBIT)	**0**
EBIT Margin	**0%**
Interest Expense	0
Profit Before Tax (PBT)	**0**
Profit Before Tax Margin	**0%**
Income Tax Expense	**0**
Profit (-Loss) After Tax (PAT)	**0**
Profit (-Loss) After Tax %	**0%**

Checks	
Equity = Net Assets	TRUE
Cash Flow Cash = Balance Sheet Cash	TRUE
P&L Retained Earnings = P&L Retained Eranings	TRUE

Balance Sheet	Period 1
As At	31-Jan-27
Assets	
Current Assets	
Cash	(1,000)
Inventory/Stock	0
Accounts Receivable	0
Prepaid Expenses	0
Total Current Assets	**(1,000)**
Fixed Assets	
Fixed Assets	0
Accumulated Depreciation	0
Total Fixed Assets	**0**
Total Assets	**(1,000)**
Current Liabilities	
Accounts Payable	1,000
Deferred Revenue	0
Accrued Employee Costs	0
Provision for Income Tax	0
Total Current Liabilities	**1,000**
Long Term Liabilities	
Bank Loans	0
Total Liabilities	**1,000**
Net Assets	**0**
Equity	
Share Capital	0
Retained Earnings b/f	0
Retained Earnings	0
Total Equity	**0**

Statement of Cash Flows	Period 1
Date From	01-Jan-27
Date To	31-Jan-27
Operating Cash	
Receipts from Customers	0
Payments to Staff	0
Payments to Suppliers	(1,000)
Loan Interest Payment	0
Income Taxes Paid	0
Net Operating Cash	**(1,000)**
Investing	
Payments for Fixed Assets	0
Financing	
Cash from Shareholders	0
Dividend Paid	0
Bank Loans Received	0
Loan Principle Repayments	0
Net Financing Cash Flow	**0**
Net Cash for The Period	**(1,000)**
Opening Cash	**0**
Closing Cash	**(1,000)**

Statement of Cash Flows

Operating Activities:
Payments to Suppliers: Reflects an outflow of $1,000 for the payment to the electricity supplier.
Net Operating Cash: Reflects an outflow of $1,000.
Net Cash for the Period: Reflects a total outflow of $1,000.
Closing Cash: The ending cash balance for the period is -$1,000, reflecting the payment made.

Income Statement

There is no direct impact on the income statement from this transaction since it involves the payment of a previously recorded liability and does not involve new revenue or expenses for the period.

Balance Sheet

Assets:
Current Assets: Cash decreases by $1,000, reflecting the payment made.
Liabilities:
Current Liabilities: Accounts Payable decreases by $1,000, reflecting the settlement of the liability.
The decrease in one current asset (cash) and the corresponding decrease in current liabilities (accounts payable) keep the accounting equation balanced: Assets = Liabilities + Equity.

Event 9.01: The Business Incurs Advertising Expenses (Invoice Received)

Event 9.01: The Business Incurs Advertising Expenses (Invoice Received)

Commercial Purpose

The commercial purpose of incurring advertising expenses is to promote the business and its products or services. This expense is necessary to attract customers, increase sales, and enhance brand awareness.

Source Documents

Advertising Invoice: Document detailing the cost of advertising services.
Payment Voucher: Document authorising the payment for advertising services.
Advertising Agreement: Contract outlining the terms and duration of the advertising campaign.

The business incurs advertising expense.

Amount	2,000.00
Date	3/01/2027

Tees and Giggles Ltd

Financial Statements

Income Statement	Period 1
Date From	01-Jan-27
Date To	31-Jan-27
Sales Revenue	0
Cost of Sales	0
Gross Profit	**0**
Gross Profit Margin %	**0%**
Expenses	
Wages Expense	0
Wages Oncosts Expense	0
Electricity Expense	0
Rent Expense	0
Advertising Expense	(2,000)
Subscription Expense	0
Depreciation Expense	0
Total Expenses	**(2,000)**
Earning Before Interest and Taxation (EBIT)	**(2,000)**
EBIT Margin	**0%**
Interest Expense	0
Profit Before Tax (PBT)	**(2,000)**
Profit Before Tax Margin	**0%**
Income Tax Expense	**0**
Profit (-Loss) After Tax (PAT)	**(2,000)**
Profit (-Loss) After Tax %	**0%**

Checks	
Equity = Net Assets	TRUE
Cash Flow Cash = Balance Sheet Cash	TRUE
P&L Retained Earnings = P&L Retained Eranings	TRUE

Balance Sheet	Period 1
As At	31-Jan-27
Assets	
Current Assets	
Cash	0
Inventory/Stock	0
Accounts Receivable	0
Prepaid Expenses	0
Total Current Assets	**0**
Fixed Assets	
Fixed Assets	0
Accumulated Depreciation	0
Total Fixed Assets	**0**
Total Assets	**0**
Current Liabilities	
Accounts Payable	(2,000)
Deferred Revenue	0
Accrued Employee Costs	0
Provision for Income Tax	0
Total Current Liabilities	**(2,000)**
Long Term Liabilities	
Bank Loans	0
Total Liabilities	**(2,000)**
Net Assets	**(2,000)**
Equity	
Share Capital	0
Retained Earnings b/f	0
Retained Earnings	(2,000)
Total Equity	**(2,000)**

Statement of Cash Flows	Period 1
Date From	01-Jan-27
Date To	31-Jan-27
Operating Cash	
Receipts from Customers	0
Payments to Staff	0
Payments to Suppliers	0
Loan Interest Payment	0
Income Taxes Paid	0
Net Operating Cash	**0**
Investing	
Payments for Fixed Assets	0
Financing	
Cash from Shareholders	0
Dividend Paid	0
Bank Loans Received	0
Loan Principle Repayments	0
Net Financing Cash Flow	**0**
Net Cash for The Period	**0**
Opening Cash	0
Closing Cash	**0**

Statement of Cash Flows

There is no immediate impact on the statement of cash flows since the expense has been incurred but not yet paid. The cash impact will be recorded when the payment is made.

Income Statement

Advertising Expense: The income statement records an advertising expense of $2,000 for the period.
Total Expenses: Reflect the addition of the advertising expense.
Profit Before Tax (PBT): Reflects a loss of $2,000 due to the advertising expense.

Balance Sheet

Liabilities:
Current Liabilities: Accounts Payable increase by $2,000, reflecting the obligation to pay the advertising supplier.
Equity:
Retained Earnings: Decrease by $2,000, reflecting the net loss from the advertising expense.
The increase in liabilities (accounts payable) and the corresponding decrease in equity (retained earnings) keep the accounting equation balanced: Assets = Liabilities + Equity.

Event 9.02: Business Pays Advertising Supplier

Event 9.02: Business Pays Advertising Supplier

Commercial Purpose

The commercial purpose of paying the advertising supplier $2,000 is to settle the outstanding accounts payable for the advertising expense previously incurred. This payment ensures that the business fulfils its obligation to the supplier and maintains a good credit relationship.

Source Documents

Payment Voucher: Document authorising the payment to the advertising supplier.
Bank Statement: Evidence of the $2,000 cash payment made to the supplier.
Advertising Invoice: Document detailing the cost of advertising services provided.

The business pays the advertising supplier.

Amount	2,000.00
Date	13/01/2027

Tees and Giggles Ltd

Financial Statements

Income Statement	Period 1
Date From	01-Jan-27
Date To	31-Jan-27
Sales Revenue	0
Cost of Sales	0
Gross Profit	**0**
Gross Profit Margin %	**0%**
Expenses	
Wages Expense	0
Wages Oncosts Expense	0
Electricity Expense	0
Rent Expense	0
Advertising Expense	0
Subscription Expense	0
Depreciation Expense	0
Total Expenses	**0**
Earning Before Interest and Taxation (EBIT)	**0**
EBIT Margin	**0%**
Interest Expense	0
Profit Before Tax (PBT)	**0**
Profit Before Tax Margin	**0%**
Income Tax Expense	**0**
Profit (-Loss) After Tax (PAT)	**0**
Profit (-Loss) After Tax %	**0%**

Checks	
Equity = Net Assets	TRUE
Cash Flow Cash = Balance Sheet Cash	TRUE
P&L Retained Earnings = P&L Retained Eranings	TRUE

Balance Sheet	Period 1
As At	31-Jan-27
Assets	
Current Assets	
Cash	(2,000)
Inventory/Stock	0
Accounts Receivable	0
Prepaid Expenses	0
Total Current Assets	**(2,000)**
Fixed Assets	
Fixed Assets	0
Accumulated Depreciation	0
Total Fixed Assets	**0**
Total Assets	**(2,000)**
Current Liabilities	
Accounts Payable	2,000
Deferred Revenue	0
Accrued Employee Costs	0
Provision for Income Tax	0
Total Current Liabilities	**2,000**
Long Term Liabilities	
Bank Loans	0
Total Liabilities	**2,000**
Net Assets	**0**
Equity	
Share Capital	0
Retained Earnings b/f	0
Retained Earnings	0
Total Equity	**0**

Statement of Cash Flows	Period 1
Date From	01-Jan-27
Date To	31-Jan-27
Operating Cash	
Receipts from Customers	0
Payments to Staff	0
Payments to Suppliers	(2,000)
Loan Interest Payment	0
Income Taxes Paid	0
Net Operating Cash	**(2,000)**
Investing	
Payments for Fixed Assets	0
Financing	
Cash from Shareholders	0
Dividend Paid	0
Bank Loans Received	0
Loan Principle Repayments	0
Net Financing Cash Flow	**0**
Net Cash for The Period	**(2,000)**
Opening Cash	**0**
Closing Cash	**(2,000)**

Statement of Cash Flows

Operating Activities:
Payments to Suppliers: Reflects an outflow of $2,000 for the payment to the advertising supplier.
Net Operating Cash: Reflects an outflow of $2,000.
Net Cash for the Period: Reflects a total outflow of $2,000.
Closing Cash: The ending cash balance for the period is -$2,000, reflecting the payment made.

Income Statement

There is no direct impact on the income statement from this transaction since it involves the payment of a previously recorded liability and does not involve new revenue or expenses for the period.

Balance Sheet

Assets:
Current Assets: Cash decreases by $2,000, reflecting the payment made.
Liabilities:
Current Liabilities: Accounts Payable decreases by $2,000, reflecting the settlement of the liability.
The decrease in one current asset (cash) and the corresponding decrease in current liabilities (accounts payable) keep the accounting equation balanced: Assets = Liabilities + Equity.

Event 10.01: The Business Receives Rent Invoice

Event 10.01: The Business Receives Rent Invoice

Commercial Purpose

The commercial purpose of recognising the rent expense is to account for the cost of leasing premises used for business operations. This expense is necessary for the business to operate in a suitable location and is typically a recurring cost.

Source Documents

Rent Invoice: Document detailing the cost of rent for the period.
Lease Agreement: Contract outlining the terms and conditions of the rental arrangement.

The business Receives Rent Invoice.

Amount	3,000.00
Date	1/01/2027

Tees and Giggles Ltd

Financial Statements

Income Statement	Period 1
Date From	01-Jan-27
Date To	31-Jan-27
Sales Revenue	0
Cost of Sales	0
Gross Profit	**0**
Gross Profit Margin %	**0%**
Expenses	
Wages Expense	0
Wages Oncosts Expense	0
Electricity Expense	0
Rent Expense	(3,000)
Advertising Expense	0
Subscription Expense	0
Depreciation Expense	0
Total Expenses	**(3,000)**
Earning Before Interest and Taxation (EBIT)	**(3,000)**
EBIT Margin	**0%**
Interest Expense	0
Profit Before Tax (PBT)	**(3,000)**
Profit Before Tax Margin	**0%**
Income Tax Expense	**0**
Profit (-Loss) After Tax (PAT)	**(3,000)**
Profit (-Loss) After Tax %	**0%**

Checks	
Equity = Net Assets	TRUE
Cash Flow Cash = Balance Sheet Cash	TRUE
P&L Retained Earnings = P&L Retained Eranings	TRUE

Balance Sheet	Period 1
As At	31-Jan-27
Assets	
Current Assets	
Cash	0
Inventory/Stock	0
Accounts Receivable	0
Prepaid Expenses	0
Total Current Assets	**0**
Fixed Assets	
Fixed Assets	0
Accumulated Depreciation	0
Total Fixed Assets	**0**
Total Assets	**0**
Current Liabilities	
Accounts Payable	(3,000)
Deferred Revenue	0
Accrued Employee Costs	0
Provision for Income Tax	0
Total Current Liabilities	**(3,000)**
Long Term Liabilities	
Bank Loans	0
Total Liabilities	**(3,000)**
Net Assets	**(3,000)**
Equity	
Share Capital	0
Retained Earnings b/f	0
Retained Earnings	(3,000)
Total Equity	**(3,000)**

Statement of Cash Flows	Period 1
Date From	01-Jan-27
Date To	31-Jan-27
Operating Cash	
Receipts from Customers	0
Payments to Staff	0
Payments to Suppliers	0
Loan Interest Payment	0
Income Taxes Paid	0
Net Operating Cash	**0**
Investing	
Payments for Fixed Assets	0
Financing	
Cash from Shareholders	0
Dividend Paid	0
Bank Loans Received	0
Loan Principle Repayments	0
Net Financing Cash Flow	**0**
Net Cash for The Period	**0**
Opening Cash	0
Closing Cash	**0**

Statement of Cash Flows

There is no immediate impact on the statement of cash flows since the expense has been incurred but not yet paid. The cash impact will be recorded when the payment is made.

Income Statement

Rent Expense: The income statement records a rent expense of $3,000 for the period.
Total Expenses: Reflect the addition of the rent expense.
Profit Before Tax (PBT): Reflects a loss of $3,000 due to the rent expense.

Balance Sheet

Liabilities:
Current Liabilities: Accounts Payable increase by $3,000, reflecting the obligation to pay the rent supplier.
Equity:
Retained Earnings: Decrease by $3,000, reflecting the net loss from the rent expense.
The increase in liabilities (accounts payable) and the corresponding decrease in equity (retained earnings) keep the accounting equation balanced: Assets = Liabilities + Equity.

Event 10.02: Business Pays Rent Supplier

Event 10.02: Business Pays Rent Supplier

Commercial Purpose

The commercial purpose of paying the rent invoice is to settle the outstanding accounts payable for the rent expense previously incurred. This payment ensures that the business fulfils its rental obligations and maintains a good relationship with the landlord.

Source Documents

Payment Voucher: Document authorising the payment to the landlord.
Bank Statement: Evidence of the $3,000 cash payment made to the landlord.
Rent Invoice: Document detailing the cost of rent for the period.

The business pays rent invoice.

Amount	3,000.00
Date	11/01/2027

Tees and Giggles Ltd

Financial Statements

Income Statement	Period 1
Date From	01-Jan-27
Date To	31-Jan-27
Sales Revenue	0
Cost of Sales	0
Gross Profit	**0**
Gross Profit Margin %	**0%**
Expenses	
Wages Expense	0
Wages Oncosts Expense	0
Electricity Expense	0
Rent Expense	0
Advertising Expense	0
Subscription Expense	0
Depreciation Expense	0
Total Expenses	**0**
Earning Before Interest and Taxation (EBIT)	**0**
EBIT Margin	**0%**
Interest Expense	0
Profit Before Tax (PBT)	**0**
Profit Before Tax Margin	**0%**
Income Tax Expense	**0**
Profit (-Loss) After Tax (PAT)	**0**
Profit (-Loss) After Tax %	**0%**

Checks	
Equity = Net Assets	TRUE
Cash Flow Cash = Balance Sheet Cash	TRUE
P&L Retained Earnings = P&L Retained Earnings	TRUE

Balance Sheet	Period 1
As At	31-Jan-27
Assets	
Current Assets	
Cash	(3,000)
Inventory/Stock	0
Accounts Receivable	0
Prepaid Expenses	0
Total Current Assets	**(3,000)**
Fixed Assets	
Fixed Assets	0
Accumulated Depreciation	0
Total Fixed Assets	**0**
Total Assets	**(3,000)**
Current Liabilities	
Accounts Payable	3,000
Deferred Revenue	0
Accrued Employee Costs	0
Provision for Income Tax	0
Total Current Liabilities	**3,000**
Long Term Liabilities	
Bank Loans	0
Total Liabilities	**3,000**
Net Assets	**0**
Equity	
Share Capital	0
Retained Earnings b/f	0
Retained Earnings	0
Total Equity	**0**

Statement of Cash Flows	Period 1
Date From	01-Jan-27
Date To	31-Jan-27
Operating Cash	
Receipts from Customers	0
Payments to Staff	0
Payments to Suppliers	(3,000)
Loan Interest Payment	0
Income Taxes Paid	0
Net Operating Cash	**(3,000)**
Investing	
Payments for Fixed Assets	0
Financing	
Cash from Shareholders	0
Dividend Paid	0
Bank Loans Received	0
Loan Principle Repayments	0
Net Financing Cash Flow	**0**
Net Cash for The Period	**(3,000)**
Opening Cash	**0**
Closing Cash	**(3,000)**

Statement of Cash Flows

Operating Activities:
Payments to Suppliers: Reflects an outflow of $3,000 for the payment to the landlord.
Net Operating Cash: Reflects an outflow of $3,000.
Net Cash for the Period: Reflects a total outflow of $3,000.
Closing Cash: The ending cash balance for the period is -$3,000, reflecting the payment made.

Income Statement

There is no direct impact on the income statement from this transaction since it involves the payment of a previously recorded liability and does not involve new revenue or expenses for the period.

Balance Sheet

Assets:
Current Assets: Cash decreases by $3,000, reflecting the payment made.
Liabilities:
Current Liabilities: Accounts Payable decreases by $3,000, reflecting the settlement of the liability.
The decrease in one current asset (cash) and the corresponding decrease in current liabilities (accounts payable) keep the accounting equation balanced: Assets = Liabilities + Equity.

Financial Statements Showing All Transactions

All Transaction Period 1

Amount	All Transactions
Date	31/01/2027

Tees and Giggles Ltd

Financial Statements

Income Statement

	Period 1
Date From	01-Jan-27
Date To	31-Jan-27
Sales Revenue	20,000
Cost of Sales	(4,000)
Gross Profit	**16,000**
Gross Profit Margin %	**80%**
Expenses	
Wages Expense	(5,000)
Wages Oncosts Expense	(1,000)
Electricity Expense	(1,000)
Rent Expense	(3,000)
Advertising Expense	(2,000)
Subscription Expense	(2,000)
Depreciation Expense	(139)
Total Expenses	**(14,139)**
Earning Before Interest and Taxation (EBIT)	**1,861**
EBIT Margin	**9%**
Interest Expense	(42)
Profit Before Tax (PBT)	**1,819**
Profit Before Tax Margin	**9%**
Income Tax Expense	**0**
Profit (-Loss) After Tax (PAT)	**1,819**
Profit (-Loss) After Tax %	**9%**

Checks

Equity = Net Assets	TRUE
Cash Flow Cash = Balance Sheet Cash	TRUE
P&L Retained Earnings = P&L Retained Eranings	TRUE

Balance Sheet

	Period 1
As At	31-Jan-27
Assets	
Current Assets	
Cash	9,561
Inventory/Stock	1,000
Accounts Receivable	0
Prepaid Expenses	22,000
Total Current Assets	**32,561**
Fixed Assets	
Fixed Assets	5,000
Accumulated Depreciation	(139)
Total Fixed Assets	**4,861**
Total Assets	**37,422**
Current Liabilities	
Accounts Payable	0
Deferred Revenue	(5,000)
Accrued Employee Costs	0
Provision for Income Tax	0
Total Current Liabilities	**(5,000)**
Long Term Liabilities	
Bank Loans	(9,603)
Total Liabilities	**(14,603)**
Net Assets	**22,819**
Equity	
Share Capital	21,000
Retained Earnings b/f	0
Retained Earnings	1,819
Total Equity	**22,819**

Statement of Cash Flows

	Period 1
Date From	01-Jan-27
Date To	31-Jan-27
Operating Cash	
Receipts from Customers	25,000
Payments to Staff	(6,000)
Payments to Suppliers	(35,000)
Loan Interest Payment	(42)
Income Taxes Paid	0
Net Operating Cash	**(16,042)**
Investing	
Payments for Fixed Assets	(5,000)
Financing	
Cash from Shareholders	21,000
Dividend Paid	0
Bank Loans Received	10,000
Loan Principle Repayments	(397)
Net Financing Cash Flow	**30,603**
Net Cash for The Period	**9,561**
Opening Cash	**0**
Closing Cash	**9,561**

Key Insights and Recommendations

Key Insights

Profitability:

The company has a strong gross profit margin of 80%, indicating effective control over the cost of goods sold.

The net profit margin of 6% is positive, but there is room for improvement by managing operating expenses more efficiently.

Liquidity:

Current assets significantly exceed current liabilities, indicating strong liquidity. The current ratio is approximately 5.87 ($32,561 / $5,546), which suggests that the company can easily cover its short-term obligations.

Solvency:

The debt-to-equity ratio is 0.68 ($15,149 / $22,273), indicating a moderate level of debt relative to equity. This suggests that the company is not overly reliant on debt financing, which is a positive sign for long-term solvency.

Cash Flow Management:

The company experienced a negative net operating cash flow of $16,042, primarily due to high payments to suppliers. It is crucial to monitor and manage these payments to ensure adequate cash flow for operations.

Positive net cash flow from financing activities ($30,603) helped to offset the negative operating cash flow, resulting in a net increase in cash of $9,561 for the period.

Recommendations:

Expense Management:

Review and manage operating expenses, particularly wages, rent, and advertising, to improve profitability.

Receivables and Payables:

Implement strategies to improve collections from customers to enhance operating cash flow. Consider negotiating better payment terms with suppliers to improve cash management.

Investment:

Ensure that investments in fixed assets are aligned with business growth and revenue generation. Monitor the depreciation of assets to maintain accurate financial records.

Debt Management:

Maintain a balanced approach to financing through equity and debt. Ensure that the interest and principal repayments are manageable relative to the company's cash flows.

By following these recommendations and closely monitoring financial performance, Tees and Giggles Ltd can improve its profitability, liquidity, and overall financial health.

Chapter 07: Skill-Building Exercises and Questions

TUse the following link to answer the following questions.

https://magicofaccounting.ecoachinghub.com/chapter7

You have been asked to evaluate the impact if the following conditions were in place.

1. Negotiate Better Terms with T-shirt supplier

Event 3. Number of units purchased: 2,000

Event 3. Cost per unit $4

Event 3. Credit Terms Days 30 Days

1. Increase Sales

Event 4. Number of T-shirts sold 1,500

Event 4: Markup on Cost 500%

Event 4: T-shirts delivered 1,200

1. Reduce Expenses

Event 6: Software subscription $18,000

Event 6: Credit terms days 30

Total Revenue

Net Profit After Tax

Total Assets

Total Liabilities

Net Assets

Net Operating Cash

Closing Cash Balance

Well done! You have learned about the necessity of accounting in tracking business transactions, maintaining financial records, and producing reports essential for various stakeholders.

Chapter 08: Ratio Analysis

Chapter 08 Objective: Understand ratio analysis and its significance in evaluating a business's financial performance, including liquidity, profitability, efficiency, and solvency ratios.

What is Ratio Analysis

Ratio analysis is a powerful tool that helps you understand the financial health of your business by examining the relationships between different financial statement items. It simplifies complex financial data into key indicators, making it easier to make informed business decisions. In this chapter, we will explain what ratio analysis is and explore the key types of ratios—**liquidity, profitability, efficiency, and solvency**—using practical examples from Tees and Giggles Ltd.

Ratio analysis involves calculating and interpreting financial ratios from your business's financial statements. These ratios provide insights into various aspects of your business's performance and financial position.

Example: Think of ratios like a health checkup for your business. Just as a doctor uses various metrics like blood pressure and cholesterol levels to assess your health, ratios help you evaluate different areas of your business's financial health.

Liquidity Ratios

Liquidity ratios measure your business's ability to meet short-term obligations. They indicate whether you have enough liquid assets (like cash) to cover your current liabilities (like bills and short-term loans).

Current Ratio:

Ratio Name		Calculation Formula		Calculation (Example from Tees and Giggles Ltd)		Ratio
Current Ratio	=	Current Assets / Current Liabilities	=	32,561 / 5,546	=	5.87

A higher current ratio indicates that the business has more than enough assets to cover its short-term liabilities. Tees and Giggles Ltd has $5.87 in current assets for every $1 of current liabilities, showing strong liquidity.

Quick Ratio:

Ratio Name		Calculation Formula		Calculation		Ratio
				Example from Tees and Giggles Ltd		
Quick Ratio	=	Current Assets - Inventory / Current Liabilities	=	32,561-1,000 / 5,546	=	5.69

The quick ratio excludes inventory from current assets, providing a more stringent test of liquidity. Tees and Giggles Ltd has quick ratios of 5.69 in Period 1, indicating that even without selling inventory, the business can comfortably meet its short-term obligations.

Cash Ratio:

Ratio Name		Calculation Formula		Calculation		Ratio
				Example from Tees and Giggles Ltd		
Cash Ratio	=	Cash / Current Liabilities	=	9,561 / 5,546	=	1.72

The cash ratio measures the business's ability to pay off short-term liabilities with cash alone. With ratio of 1.72 in Periods 1. Tees and Giggles Ltd is in a good position to cover its current liabilities with cash.

Profitability Ratios

Profitability ratios assess your ability to generate profit relative to sales, assets, and equity. These ratios show how efficiently your business is at making money.

Gross Profit Margin:

Ratio Name		Calculation Formula		Calculation (Example from Tees and Giggles Ltd)		Ratio
Gross Profit Margin	=	$\frac{\text{Gross Profit}}{\text{Revenue}} \times 100$	=	$\frac{16{,}000}{20{,}000} \times 100$	=	80%

A high gross profit margin indicates efficient production and strong pricing power. Tees and Giggles Ltd consistently retains 80% of its sales as gross profit, showing robust profitability before operating expenses.

Net Profit Margin:

Ratio Name		Calculation Formula		Calculation (Example from Tees and Giggles Ltd)		Ratio
Net Profit Margin	=	$\frac{\text{Net Profit *}}{\text{Revenue}} \times 100$	=	$\frac{1{,}273}{20{,}000} \times 100$	=	6%

Net profit margin shows the percentage of revenue that remains as profit after all expenses. 6% in Period 1 indicates that the company is profitable.

Return on Assets Ratio (ROA):

Ratio Name		Calculation Formula		Calculation (Example from Tees and Giggles Ltd)		Ratio
Return on Assets (ROA)	=	$\frac{\text{Net Profit *}}{\text{Total Assets}} \times 100$	=	$\frac{1,273}{37,422} \times 100$	=	3%

* Net Profit = Profit (-Loss) After Tax (PAT)

ROA measures how effectively the company uses its assets to generate profit. 3% suggests that the company's assets are generating a profit.

Return on Equity (ROE) Ratio:

Ratio Name		Calculation Formula		Calculation (Example from Tees and Giggles Ltd)		Ratio
Return on Equity (ROE)	=	$\frac{\text{Net Profit *}}{\text{Shareholders' Equity}} \times 100$	=	$\frac{1,273}{22,273} \times 100$	=	6%

* Net Profit = Profit (-Loss) After Tax (PAT)

ROE indicates how well the company generates profit from shareholders' equity.

6% shows a return in profitability relative to equity.

Efficiency Ratios

Efficiency ratios evaluate how well you manage your assets and liabilities to generate sales and maximise profits.

Inventory Turnover:

Ratio Name		Calculation Formula		Calculation		Ratio
				Example from Tees and Giggles Ltd		
Inventory Turnover	=	Cost of Goods Sold / Average Inventory	=	4,000 / 3,000	=	1.33

Opening Inventory =	5,000
Closign Inventory =	1,000
Average Inventory =	3,000

A higher inventory turnover ratio indicates efficient inventory management.

Receivable Turnover:

Ratio Name		Calculation Formula		Calculation		Ratio
				Example from Tees and Giggles Ltd		
Receivables Turnover	=	Net Credit Sales / Average Accounts Receiveble	=	25,000 / 12,500	=	2.00

Opening Accounts Receivable =	25,000
Closing Accounts Receivable =	-
Average Accounts Receivable =	12,500

A consistent receivables turnover ratio indicates stable efficiency in collecting payments from customers.

Payables Turnover:

Ratio Name		Calculation Formula		Calculation		Ratio
				Example from Tees and Giggles Ltd		
Payables Turnover	=	Net Credit Purchases / Average Accounts Payable	=	40,000 / 20,000	=	2.00

Opening Accounts Payable =	40,000
Closing Accounts Payable =	-
Average Accounts Payable =	20,000

A consistent payables turnover ratio indicates stable efficiency in paying off suppliers.

Asset Turnover:

Ratio Name		Calculation Formula		Calculation		Ratio
				Example from Tees and Giggles Ltd		
Asset Turnover	=	Revenue / Average Total Assets	=	20,000 / 37,422	=	0.53

An increasing asset turnover ratio indicates efficient use of assets to generate revenue.

Solvency Ratios

Solvency ratios measure your business's ability to meet long-term obligations. They provide insight into your business's financial stability and risk level.

Debt to Equity Ratio:

Ratio Name		Calculation Formula		Calculation (Example from Tees and Giggles Ltd)		Ratio
Debt to Equity Ratio	=	Total Liabilities / Shareholders' Equity	=	15,149 / 22,273	=	0.68

A higher debt to equity ratio indicates greater reliance on debt financing, which may increase financial risk.

Interest Cover Ratio:

Ratio Name		Calculation Formula		Calculation (Example from Tees and Giggles Ltd)		Ratio
Interest Cover	=	EBIT* / Interest Expense	=	1,861 / 42	=	44.31

* EBIT = Earnings Before Interest and Tax

A high interest coverage ratio indicates that the company can comfortably cover its interest expenses. Tees and Giggles Ltd maintains a strong interest coverage ratio above 40, suggesting low financial risk related to interest payments.

Ratios Conclusion

Ratio analysis provides a comprehensive picture of a business's financial health. By regularly calculating and interpreting these ratios, you can gain valuable insights into liquidity, profitability, efficiency, and solvency. For Tees and Giggles Ltd, the analysis reveals strong liquidity, consistent profitability, improving efficiency, and manageable solvency, with some areas for further improvement. Understanding and utilising these ratios will help you make informed decisions to drive your business towards greater success.

Multiple Choice Questions for Chapter 8: Ratio Analysis, Answers and Explanations are in Appendix 4.

Question 1: Which ratio measures a company's ability to cover its short-term liabilities with its most liquid assets?

A. Current Ratio

B. Quick Ratio

C. Cash Ratio

D. Return on Assets (ROA)

Question 2: What does a high gross profit margin indicate?

A. Efficient inventory management

B. Effective control over the cost of goods sold

C. Ability to cover short-term liabilities with cash

D. Efficient use of assets to generate profit

Question 3: Which ratio evaluates how well a company uses its assets to generate revenue?

A. Current Ratio

B. Quick Ratio

C. Asset Turnover Ratio

D. Debt to Equity Ratio

Question 4: Which of the following ratios would you use to assess a company's long-term financial stability and risk level?

A. Liquidity Ratios

B. Profitability Ratios

C. Efficiency Ratios

D. Solvency Ratios

Question 5: If Tees and Giggles Ltd has a debt-to-equity ratio of 0.68, what does this indicate?

A. High liquidity

B. Strong profitability

C. Moderate level of debt relative to equity

D. High financial risk related to interest payments

Well done! You learned about ratio analysis and its importance in evaluating various aspects of a business's financial performance using liquidity, profitability, efficiency, and solvency ratios.

Part 3 – Tax, Governance, and Accountability in Business

Accounting isn't just about keeping score; it's about playing by the rules. In this part, you'll learn how taxes, governance, and accountability intersect with accounting to keep businesses on the right track. Whether it's understanding tax obligations, implementing corporate governance, or upholding the responsibilities of business owners, this part equips you with the knowledge to navigate the regulatory landscape. It's all about ensuring that your business is not just profitable, but also compliant and responsible.

Chapter 09: Tax and Accounting

Chapter 09 Objective: Learn about the intersection of tax and accounting, including tax rules, record-keeping, taxable income, tax penalties, and the role of tax accountants.

Taxes are an essential part of running a business. Understanding tax rules and how they intersect with accounting can help you comply with regulations and avoid penalties. In this chapter, we will cover key aspects of tax and accounting, including tax rules, record keeping, taxable income, the role of tax accountants, tax penalties, and tax audits.

Tax Rules

Tax rules are the laws and regulations that govern how businesses and individuals must calculate and pay taxes. These rules vary by country and can be complex.

Key Points:

Income Tax: Businesses pay taxes on their Taxable Profits (Income), which is the income remaining after deducting allowable expenses.

Some types of expenses are disallowed as deductions for tax purposes. Examples are:

Personal Expenses: Any expenses that are personal in nature and not related to business operations, such as personal travel, personal meals, and clothing (unless it is a uniform).

Fines and Penalties: Any fines or penalties imposed by the government or regulatory authorities, including traffic fines, environmental penalties, and other similar charges.

Capital Expenditures: Costs incurred for acquiring, improving, or upgrading fixed assets, such as buildings, machinery, and equipment. These expenses must be capitalised and depreciated over time instead of being immediately deducted. Tax depreciation rates are sometime mandated by Tax authorities, unlike for accounting, where depreciation rates can be set by companies.

Entertainment Expenses: Costs related to entertaining clients or employees that are deemed excessive or lavish, such as luxury events, golf outings, and expensive meals, are often disallowed or limited.

Illegal Payments and Bribes: Any payments made that are illegal, such as bribes or kickbacks, are not deductible.

Your tax accountant will be fully aware of tax rules applicable in your country.

Sales Tax / GST / VAT: Collected on sales of goods and services and remitted to the government.

Payroll Tax: Taxes on wages paid to employees, including Social Security, Pensions, Superannuation Etc.

Record Keeping, accounting records can be used

Accounting Records Can Be Used

Good record keeping is crucial for tax purposes. Accurate and organized records ensure you can substantiate your income and expenses, which is essential for accurate tax reporting.

Key Records:

Sales Records: Invoices, receipts, and sales journals.

Expense Records: Receipts, bills, and expense reports.

Payroll Records: Employee wages, benefits, and tax withholdings.

Example:

If your bakery spends $2,000 on ingredients, you need to keep receipts to prove this expense when claiming deductions on your tax return.

Taxable Income

Taxable income is the portion of your income subject to tax, calculated by subtracting allowable deductions from your gross income.

Example:

If your business's total Accounting Profit is $150,000 and you have $50,000 in disallowable expenses, your Taxable Income is $200,000.

Tax Accountants

Tax accountants are professionals who specialise in tax law and tax preparation. They can help you navigate the complexities of tax rules, ensure compliance, and optimise your tax situation.

Key Services:

Tax Preparation: Filing tax returns accurately and on time.

Tax Planning: Advising on tax-saving strategies and planning for future tax liabilities.

Audit Representation: Assisting during tax audits by representing your interests.

Example:

A tax accountant might help your business identify deductions you were unaware of, such as home office expenses if you manage your business from home.

Tax Penalties

Tax penalties are fines imposed by tax authorities for failing to comply with tax rules. Common reasons for penalties include late filing, underpayment of taxes, and inaccurate information.

Key Penalties:

Late Filing Penalty: Fines for not submitting your tax return by the due date.

Late Payment Penalty: Charges for not paying your taxes owed by the deadline.

Accuracy-Related Penalty: Fines for errors or underreporting income on your tax return.

Example:

If your business owes $10,000 in taxes and you file your return two months late, you could face a penalty of 5% per month, resulting in a $1,000 penalty.

Tax Audits

A tax audit is an examination of your tax return by the tax authorities to verify accuracy and compliance. Audits can be random or triggered by discrepancies or red flags in your tax return.

Key Points:

Types of Audits: Correspondence audit (handled by mail) and field audit (conducted at your business premises).

Preparation: Maintain organized records and respond promptly and accurately to audit inquiries.

Example:

If your business reports significantly higher deductions than similar businesses, the tax authorities might audit you to ensure these deductions are legitimate.

Chapter 09: Skill-Building Exercises and Questions

Exercise 1: Research and list the types of taxes your business is subject to. Include income tax, GST/VAT/Sales tax, and payroll tax.

Exercise 2: Create a checklist of essential records you need to keep for tax purposes. Ensure you cover sales records, expense records, and payroll records.

Create a checklist of essential records you need to keep for tax purposes. Ensure you cover sales records, expense records, and payroll records.

Exercise 3: Calculating Taxable Income

Using the following information, calculate your taxable income: Accounting Proifit: $120,000, Disallowed entertainment expenses: $40,000

Well done! You explored the relationship between tax and accounting, including understanding tax rules, record-keeping, taxable income, penalties, and the role of tax accountants.

Chapter 10: Responsibilities of Business Owners and Directors

Chapter 10 Objective: Understand the critical responsibilities of business owners and directors, including ensuring solvency and understanding the penalties for failing to meet legal obligations.

Running a business comes with significant responsibilities, especially for business owners and directors. These responsibilities ensure that the business operates legally, ethically, and sustainably. This chapter will focus on the critical responsibilities of business owners and directors, including ensuring solvency and understanding the penalties for directors who fail to meet their obligations.

Business must be solvent

A key responsibility of business owners and directors is to ensure that the business remains solvent. Solvency means that the business can meet its long-term financial obligations and pay its debts as they come due.

Key Points:

Assessing Solvency: Regularly review financial statements to ensure that assets exceed liabilities and that the business can cover its debts.

Maintaining Solvency: Implement sound financial management practices, such as effective cash flow management, budgeting, and cost control.

Legal Obligations: In many jurisdictions, directors have a legal duty to avoid trading while insolvent. This means not incurring debts when there is no reasonable expectation that the business can repay them.

Example:

If your business owes $50,000 in loans and accounts payable but only has $30,000 in assets, you are not solvent. You need to either increase your assets or decrease your liabilities to ensure the business can continue operating.

Penalties for Directors

Directors who fail to meet their responsibilities can face serious penalties. These penalties can be financial, legal, or reputational and can impact both the individual director and the business.

Key Penalties:

Financial Penalties: Directors can be personally liable for the debts of the company if they allow it to trade while insolvent. They may be required to compensate creditors out of their own pockets.

Legal Consequences: Directors can face fines, disqualification from serving as a director, or even imprisonment for breaches of their duties, such as fraud, negligence, or failure to comply with statutory requirements.

Reputational Damage: Being penalized as a director can harm one's professional reputation, making it difficult to secure future directorships or business opportunities.

Example:

In 2019, the directors of Carillion, a large UK construction company, faced significant scrutiny and potential penalties after the company collapsed with massive debts, highlighting failures in financial oversight and management 【source: The Guardian, "Carillion collapse: inquiry calls for directors to face penalties," 2019.

Well done! You learned about the key responsibilities of business owners and directors, focusing on ensuring business solvency and understanding legal obligations and penalties.

Chapter 11: Corporate Governance and Controls

Chapter 11 Objective: Explore the principles of corporate governance and the importance of internal controls, including delegations of authority, segregation of duties, and system access controls.

Corporate governance refers to the system of rules, practices, and processes by which a company is directed and controlled. Effective corporate governance ensures that a company operates efficiently, transparently, and ethically, safeguarding the interests of all stakeholders. This chapter will focus on key aspects of corporate governance and the controls put in place to ensure its effectiveness, including delegations of authority, segregation of duties, and system access controls.

What is Corporate Governance?

Corporate governance is the framework that guides the internal and external mechanisms of a company's operations. It balances the interests of various stakeholders, including shareholders, management, customers, suppliers, financiers, government, and the community. Effective corporate governance promotes accountability, fairness, and transparency in a company's relationship with all its stakeholders.

Delegations of Authority

Delegations of authority refer to the process of assigning decision-making powers and responsibilities to various levels within an organization. This ensures that decisions are made by the most appropriate individuals and that the board can focus on strategic oversight.

Key Points:

Efficiency: Delegating authority speeds up decision-making by empowering managers and employees to act within their designated limits.

Accountability: Clearly defined authority levels ensure that individuals are accountable for their decisions and actions.

Example: In a business, the store manager may have the authority to order supplies up to $5,000, while larger purchases require approval from the owner.

Internal Controls: Segregation of Duties

Segregation of Duties is a critical internal control mechanism designed to prevent fraud and errors by distributing tasks and responsibilities among multiple individuals. This approach ensures that no single person controls all aspects of any critical business process, thereby enhancing the reliability and integrity of financial and operational activities.

Key Points:

Fraud Prevention: By separating duties such as authorisation, custody, and record-keeping, the risk of fraudulent activities is significantly reduced. When different individuals are responsible for these tasks, it becomes difficult for any one person to manipulate the process for personal gain.

Error Detection: Having different individuals perform various tasks increases the likelihood that errors will be detected and corrected. This system of checks and balances ensures that mistakes are caught early and can be addressed promptly.

Example: In a bakery, the person who approves purchase orders should not be the same person who processes payments and reconciles bank statements. By segregating these duties, the bakery minimizes the risk of fraud and enhances the accuracy of its financial records.

Implementation:

Authorization: One individual should be responsible for authorizing transactions.

Custody: Another individual should handle the custody of assets involved in the transactions.

Record-Keeping: A different person should maintain the records of the transactions.

Reconciliation: Yet another person should be responsible for reconciling accounts and reviewing records for discrepancies.

By implementing Segregation of Duties, organizations can establish a robust internal control environment that protects assets, ensures accurate reporting, and promotes operational efficiency.

System Access Controls

System access controls are security measures that regulate who can access certain information and perform specific actions within an organization's information systems. These controls are crucial for protecting sensitive data and ensuring that only authorized personnel can perform certain tasks.

Key Points:

Data Security: Protecting sensitive information from unauthorized access reduces the risk of data breaches.

Operational Integrity: Ensuring that system functions are performed only by authorized users helps maintain accurate and reliable data.

Example: In a bakery's accounting system, only the accountant should have access to modify financial records, while other employees may only view relevant information.

Chapter 11: Skill-Building Exercises and Questions

Exercise 1: Understanding Delegations of Authority

Identify the delegation of authority in your business or a business you know. Write down the levels of authority for different roles and how decisions are made.

Exercise 2: Applying Segregation of Duties

List the key tasks in your business's financial processes, such as approving expenses, processing payments, and reconciling accounts. Explain how these tasks are or could be separated among different individuals.

Exercise 3: Implementing System Access Controls

Review the system access controls in place for your business. Identify which employees have access to different parts of your information systems and ensure that access levels are appropriate for their roles.

Well done! You understood the principles of corporate governance and the importance of internal controls, including delegations of authority, segregation of duties, and system access controls.

Part 4 – Appendices

This final part is your treasure trove of resources. From a glossary of accounting terms to lists of key professional accounting bodies, this section is designed to be your go-to reference. It also includes multiple-choice question answers to test your understanding, making sure you're well-prepared to apply what you've learned. It's the perfect way to round off your journey, leaving you with the tools you need to master the magic of accounting.

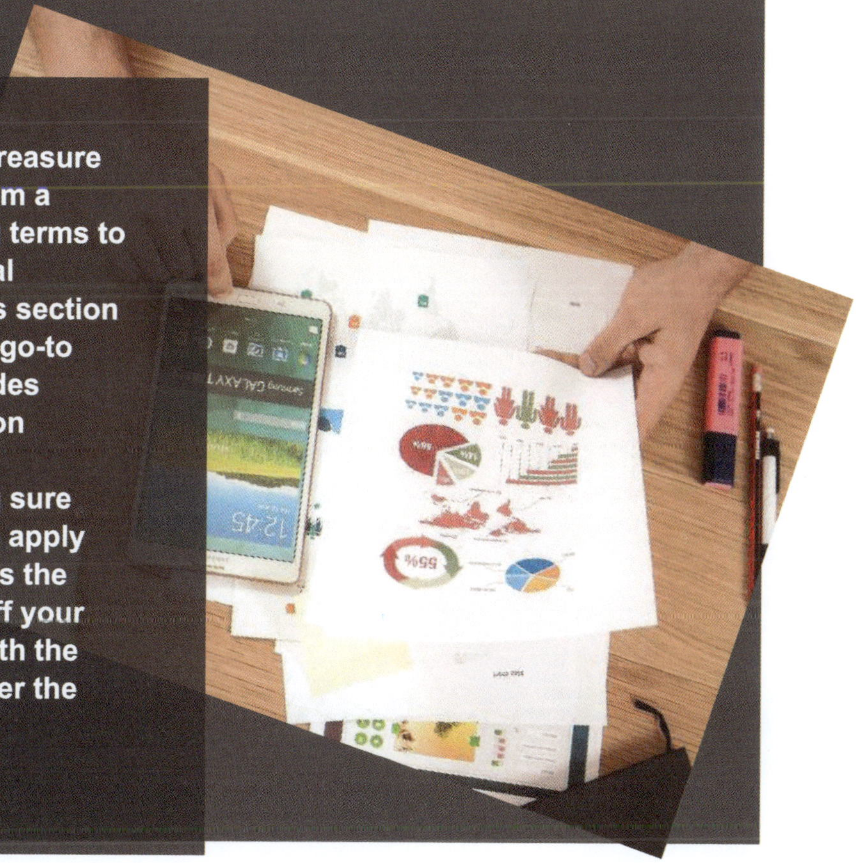

Appendix 01: Accounting Terminology Used in this Book.

A

Accrual Accounting: A method of accounting where transactions are recorded when they are earned or incurred, not when cash is exchanged.

Accrued Expenses: Expenses that have been incurred but not yet paid.

Adjusting Entries: Entries made at the end of an accounting period to update the accounts and reflect accurate balances.

Assets: Resources owned by a business that have economic value and can provide future benefits.

B

Balance Sheet: A financial statement that shows a company's financial position at a specific point in time, detailing assets, liabilities, and equity.

Bank Statement: An official summary of financial transactions in a bank account over a given period.

C

Cash Accounting: A simple accounting method where revenues and expenses are recorded only when cash is received or paid.

Chart of Accounts: A list of all accounts used by a business, categorised into assets, liabilities, equity, revenues, and expenses.

Cost of Goods Sold (COGS): The direct costs attributable to the production of the goods sold by a company.

D

Depreciation: The systematic allocation of the cost of a tangible asset over its useful life.

Double Entry System: An accounting system where every transaction affects at least two accounts, maintaining the accounting equation (Assets = Liabilities + Equity).

E

Equity: The owner's residual interest in the assets of a business after deducting liabilities.

Expenses: The costs incurred by a business in the process of earning revenue.

F

Financial Statements: Reports that summarise the financial performance and position of a business, including the income statement, balance sheet, and cash flow statement.

G

GAAP (Generally Accepted Accounting Principles): A set of accounting standards and principles used in the United States to ensure consistency and comparability in financial reporting.

Going Concern Concept: The assumption that a business will continue to operate indefinitely unless there is evidence to suggest otherwise.

I

IFRS (International Financial Reporting Standards): A set of global accounting standards that ensure consistency and comparability in financial reporting across different countries.

Income Statement: A financial statement that shows the business's performance over a specific period, detailing revenues, expenses, and the resulting profit or loss.

Inventory: The goods and materials a business holds for the purpose of resale.

L

Liabilities: Obligations of a business that it must settle in the future, such as loans and accounts payable.

M

Matching Concept: An accounting principle that requires expenses to be recorded in the same period as the revenues they help generate.

Materiality Concept: The principle that all significant information that could influence the decision-making process of users should be recorded and reported.

P

Prepaid Expenses: Payments made in advance for goods or services to be received in the future.

Profit Before Tax (PBT): The profit a company makes before income tax expenses are deducted.

Profit Margin: A measure of profitability calculated as net income divided by revenue.

R

Revenue: The income generated from normal business operations, such as sales of goods or services.

S

Sales Invoice: A document issued by a seller to a buyer detailing the sale and the amount due.

Statement of Cash Flows: A financial statement that tracks the flow of cash in and out of a business over a period, highlighting operating, investing, and financing activities.

T

Trial Balance: A bookkeeping report that lists the balances of all ledger accounts of a business at a specific point in time to check the accuracy of bookkeeping entries.

Appendix 02: Key Professional Accounting Bodies

List of Major Accounting Bodies by Country.

Australia:

CPA Australia, cpaaustralia.com.au

Chartered Accountants Australia and New Zealand (CA ANZ), charteredaccountantsanz.com

Institute of Public Accountants (IPA), publicaccountants.org.au

Canada:

Chartered Professional Accountants of Canada (CPA Canada), cpacanada.ca

Global:

International Federation of Accountants (IFAC), ifac.org

International Accounting Standards Board (IASB), ifrs.org

India:

Institute of Chartered Accountants of India (ICAI), icai.org

United Kingdom:

Institute of Chartered Accountants in England and Wales (ICAEW), icaew.com

Chartered Institute of Management Accountants (CIMA), cimaglobal.com

Association of Chartered Certified Accountants (ACCA), accaglobal.com

United States:

American Institute of Certified Public Accountants (AICPA), aicpa.org

Institute of Management Accountants (IMA), imanet.org

Financial Accounting Standards Board (FASB), fasb.org

Appendix 03: Sources and References

https://www.ifrs.org/issued-standards/list-of-standards/conceptual-framework/

https://www.investopedia.com

https://www.accountingtools.com

Appendix 04: Multiple Choice Question Answers

Chapter 01:

Explanation: Correct Answer: C. To maintain proper financial records and produce reports for stakeholders

In the context of Chapter 01: Need for Accounting, the primary reason Jim needs accounting for his T-shirt business is to maintain proper financial records and produce reports for stakeholders. Accounting is crucial for tracking all business transactions, which include sales, purchases, expenses, and other financial activities. Proper accounting ensures that the business can provide accurate and transparent financial information to various stakeholders such as regulators, customers, suppliers, financial institutions, and the business itself. This information is vital for decision-making, regulatory compliance, and assessing the financial health of the business.

Why the other options are incorrect:

A. To track the bank interest on his savings: While tracking bank interest might be relevant for personal finance, it is not the primary reason for accounting in a business context. Accounting in a business setting focuses more on comprehensive financial records and reporting.

B. To easily determine the number of T-shirts he sold: Although tracking sales is a part of accounting, it is only one aspect. The primary purpose of accounting is broader and includes maintaining overall financial records and reporting for stakeholders.

D. To avoid paying taxes: This is not the purpose of accounting. Proper accounting helps ensure compliance with tax laws, but it is not intended to avoid paying taxes. Instead, it helps in accurate tax reporting and financial transparency.

Chapter 03:

1. (B) Balance Sheet provides a snapshot of the business's financial position at a specific point in time, showing what the business owns (assets), what it owes (liabilities), and the owners' equity.

2. (C) Income Statement shows the business's performance over a specific period, detailing revenues, expenses, and the resulting profit or loss.

3. (C) Cash Flow Statement tracks the flow of cash in and out of the business over a period, highlighting operating, investing, and financing activities.

4. (B) Investors use financial statements to evaluate profitability and growth potential, helping them make informed investment decisions.

5. (C) Balance Sheet typically includes assets (what the business owns), liabilities (what the business owes), and equity (owners' interest in the business).

Chapter 06:

1. (B) The Going Concern Concept assumes that a business will continue to operate for the foreseeable future. This concept is fundamental to the preparation of financial statements as it influences the valuation of assets and liabilities. If a business is not considered a going concern, its assets might be valued at liquidation prices rather than their ongoing operational value.

2.Matching Concept (B) The Matching Concept states that expenses should be recorded in the same period as the revenues they help generate. This ensures that the financial statements accurately reflect the true profitability of a business within a specific period. For example, the cost of goods sold should be matched with the revenue from sales in the same accounting period.

3. Money Measurement Concept (B) The Money Measurement Concept dictates that only transactions which can be measured in monetary terms are recorded in the accounting records. This excludes non-quantifiable items such as employee morale or customer satisfaction, focusing instead on measurable financial transactions like sales and purchases.

4. Prudence Concept (C) The Prudence Concept, also known as the Conservatism Concept, requires accountants to record expenses and losses as soon as they are known, but revenues and profits only when they are assured of being realized. This conservative approach ensures that the financial statements do not overstate the financial position or performance of the business.

5. Entity Concept (B) The Entity Concept, or Business Entity Concept, stipulates that the business is treated as a separate entity distinct from its owner(s). This separation means that the financial transactions of the business are recorded separately from the personal transactions of the owner(s). This is crucial for accurate financial reporting and legal purposes.

Chapter 08:

Question 1: Answer: B. Quick Ratio Explanation: The quick ratio excludes inventory from current assets, providing a more stringent test of liquidity, ensuring the company can meet its short-term obligations without relying on inventory sales.

Question 2: Answer: B. Effective control over the cost of goods sold Explanation: A high gross profit margin indicates efficient production and strong pricing power, meaning the company retains a significant portion of its sales as gross profit before operating expenses.

Question 3: Answer: C. Asset Turnover Ratio Explanation: The asset turnover ratio measures how effectively the company uses its assets to generate revenue, with a higher ratio indicating more efficient use of assets.

Question 4: Answer: D. Solvency Ratios Explanation: Solvency ratios measure a business's ability to meet long-term obligations and provide insight into its financial stability and risk level.

Question 5: Answer: C. Moderate level of debt relative to equity Explanation: A debt-to-equity ratio of 0.68 suggests that the company has a moderate level of debt compared to its equity, indicating it is not overly reliant on debt financing.

> *Accounting is the language of business.*
>
> — Warren Buffett

Printed in Dunstable, United Kingdom

91223681R00067